A TRAVEL GUIDE TO

Captain James Cook's
NEW ZEALAND

A TRAVEL GUIDE TO

Captain James Cook's
NEW ZEALAND

Exploring significant locations from Cook's voyages of discovery

GRAEME LAY

NEW
HOLLAND

CONTENTS

Captain James Cook RN

INTRODUCTION

The names 'James Cook' and 'New Zealand' will always be entwined. Although not the first European to discover New Zealand—that distinction went to Dutchman Abel Tasman, in 1642—it was Lieutenant James Cook of Britain's Royal Navy who first put the whole of New Zealand on the map.

This book depicts in words, maps and photographs, the places of special importance which James Cook visited or witnessed, first in HMS *Endeavour* in 1769–70, then in HMS *Resolution* in 1773 and 1777. The places are first described as they are today, then as they were when the English navigator called by nearly 250 years ago. Places of special interest which Cook saw but was not able to linger over are also described in detail.

Fortuitously for Cook, and for today's traveller, these places are some of the most attractive destinations in New Zealand. This guide will point them out to the reader, illustrate their features and explain in detail their connections with the renowned English explorer.

Cook was commander of HM Bark *Endeavour*, which sailed from Plymouth harbour, England, in August 1768 with a crew of 94 men. The principal purpose of the voyage was for Cook and his astronomer, Charles Green, to observe a rare cosmic event, a transit of the planet Venus across the face of the sun, on 3 June 1769. Accurately observing and recording this transit would enable scholars to calculate more accurately the distance between the Earth and the Sun. This in turn would enable a more accurate calculation of longitude, something which had challenged navigators for centuries. To be able to fix longitudinal positions with precision would greatly increase the accuracy of sea charts and hence the safety of ocean voyaging.

Astronomers had calculated that the best place on Earth to observe the 3 June 1769 transit of Venus would be from somewhere in the centre of the 'South Sea', as it was then known. Fortuitously, in 1767 another English naval commander, Captain Samuel Wallis, had come upon a previously uncharted high island in the South Sea. He named it 'King George's Island' and it comprised an ideal location for observing the 1769 transit. The island later became known by its traditional name, 'Tahiti'.

Endeavour's voyage to Tahiti was made via Madeira, Rio de Janeiro and Cape Horn. The ship arrived at the island on 13 April, 1769.

Cook and Green successfully observed the transit of Venus on 3 June, from a promontory on Tahiti they named 'Point Venus'. But the expedition was far from over. Cook had been given a second set of secret instructions from the British Admiralty. He was to sail from Tahiti as far south as latitude 40°, to ascertain if a-yet undiscovered continent—named Terra Australis Incognita—lay deep in the Southern Ocean.

Cook came upon no such landmass.

Further to the his instructions, Cook was now to take *Endeavour* west, to chart the islands Abel Tasman had come upon but was not able to go ashore on, in December 1642. The Dutch had named this land 'New Zealand'. Tasman's men had seen and sketchily charted only the west coast and the north-west corner of the South Island of New Zealand. It was conceivable, European men of science thought, that this land could be Terra Australis Incognita, the Great Southern Continent.

In the late eighteenth century New Zealand was already settled, by seafaring migrants from Eastern Polynesia, who had lived on the islands since about 1300 AD. They were the descendants of people who had their origins in south-east Asia. Travelling over thousands of years, they filtered east from island to island through the Bismarck Archipelago, the Admiralty Islands and the Solomon Archipelago. By about 1200 BC their voyaging migrations had taken them throughout the cultural spheres known today as Melanesia, Micronesia and Polynesia.

Ocean-going people skilled at building large, double-hulled canoes and navigating them by star and sea patterns, these people spread through the islands, settling on some and moving on to others. Eventually the migrants reached the settlement extent of what became known as the 'Polynesian Triangle', a huge ocean sphere whose apexes were the Hawaiian archipelago in the north, Easter Island in the east and New Zealand in the south.

New Zealand was the last landmass on Earth to be settled by human beings, following its discovery by the seafaring Polynesians some time during the fourteenth century.

By the eighteenth century the people who discovered New Zealand had spread throughout its two main islands and many offshore ones. Over about 400 years they had skilfully adapted a way of life suitable to the cooler, much larger land than the tropical islands of their origin. A new culture had evolved, similar to but distinctive from that of the islands of Eastern Polynesia. From an initial hunting and gathering society these Maori people now lived in settled tribal groups and sub-groups (iwi and hapu). They cultivated crops of kumara, yams and fernroot, a diet supplemented with fresh green vegetables and the flesh of birds, fish and shellfish.

From his observations of their settlements in 1769–70, James Cook estimated that the Maori population totalled approximately 100,000. Contemporary demographers agree that this total is probably correct, although historian Michael King claims that 'a slightly higher figure, 110,000, seems more likely'.[1]

Populations of Maori were concentrated in regions of mild climate such as the north and east of Te Ika A Maui—the North Island—where the staple root crops would grow. Coastal settlements depended on supplies of fish caught on hook and line and in nets of woven flax leaves, and the plentiful shellfish. Visiting parties of Maori travelled to the far south of Te Wai Pounamu—the South Island—in search of precious jade—pounamu—from which were fashioned tools and bodily ornaments. Other prized resources such as obsidian and basalt, used for cutting tools, were mined then traded over wide areas of both main islands.

By 1769 no Europeans had set foot on the islands of New Zealand. However James Cook had read a translation of Tasman's journal and so was aware that by sailing towards New Zealand from the western Pacific he should make landfall somewhere on its east coast.

On October 6 1769, Nicholas Young, the youngest person aboard *Endeavour*, saw land from the ship's masthead—a long range of mountains, a forested plain and a wide bay. Cook recorded the appearance of New Zealand in his journal with these words:

Gentle breezes between the ENE and north, clear weather. At 5pm seeing the opening of a Bay that appear'd to run pretty far inland, hauled our wind and stood in for it...We saw in the Bay several canoes, People upon the shore and some houses in the Country. The land on the Sea-Coast is high with steep white cliffs and back inland are very high mountains, the face of the Country is of a hilly surface and appeares to be cloathed with wood and Verdure.[2]

For the next six months Cook took *Endeavour* right around New Zealand's very long coastline. He surveyed both its main islands and gave English names to places of geographical significance, landmarks that Maori had long had their own names for.

Sailing first along the east coast of the North Island, Cook then took *Endeavour* across the Bay of Plenty to the Coromandel Peninsula. There another less rare cosmic event, a transit of Mercury, was observed, on 9 November 1769. The ship then continued north to the Bay of Islands, around the northern tip of the North Island and down its west coast. After a provedoring stop at Ship Cove in Queen Charlotte Sound, *Endeavour* was taken down the east coast of the South Island, around the south of Stewart Island and up the west coast, before returning to the north-west of the South Island.

This circumnavigation disproved the theory that New Zealand was a Great Southern Continent. Instead the country consisted of two large islands and many smaller ones.

Cook and *Endeavour* left New Zealand at the end of February 1770. Naming the landform near their point of departure 'Cape Farewell', he then sailed into what was later called the Tasman Sea and thence to the east coast of Australia, then called 'New Holland'.

The chart Cook produced from his mainly running survey of

the principal islands of New Zealand is remarkably accurate for its time. And whenever he went ashore to provision his ship, he made contact with the local Maori people, and trade between the two ensued.

After Cook's first landing at Turanganui-Poverty Bay, several Maori were shot. The fatalities were caused mainly by cultural misunderstandings between the two very different peoples. Thereafter, the majority of meetings between *Endeavour*'s men and Maori were amicable.

Cook and the civilian scientists on *Endeavour,* such as Joseph Banks, showed great interest in Maori life and customs. And for their part, most Maori admired and respected Cook, recognising him as a person of great mana. This was particularly so in Tolaga Bay, Mercury Bay and Queen Charlotte Sound. One hundred and fifty years after Cook's visits to New Zealand, the eminent Maori anthropologist Te Rangi Hiroa, Sir Peter Buck, spoke of him as "'to tatau tipuna, ko Kapene Kuki"—our ancestor, Captain Cook.'[3]

Cook returned twice more to New Zealand, while on two further world voyages. These visits were principally to provision his ships while en route to other South Pacific destinations such as the Society Islands (today French Polynesia), the New Hebrides (today Vanuatu) and the Friendly Islands (now Tonga).

The primary source for accounts of Cook's time in New Zealand is his journal. As with all ship's commanders, maintaining a daily log was mandatory. Reading Cook's journals the reader is struck by how phlegmatic and unemotional the entries are. Wind, clouds, sea, latitude, longitude and the nature of harbour bottoms rule. Well, Cook was a dour north Yorkshireman after all. In contrast, the journals of the naturalist Joseph Banks, a sophisticated Londoner, are colourful. They exude a sense of wonder at the exoticness he finds himself immersed in. So, from Cook we get facts; from Banks we get feelings. And together they give us a pretty full picture. The quotations in the book are taken from Beaglehole's editions of Cook's and Banks's journals.

Cook's visits to New Zealand are marked mainly by the placenames he gave to many of the islands' geographic features, from North Cape in the North Island to Dusky Sound in the South Island. Later European arrivals named landmarks in Cook's honour, such as Cook Channel in Dusky Sound, Cook Bluff in Mercury Bay and Cook's Cove in Tolaga Bay. Striking monuments to Cook have been erected in places of special significance during his visits, in Gisborne, Mercury Bay and Ship Cove.

The portrait of James Cook, painted by Nathaniel Dance in London in 1776, appeared on New Zealand's postage stamps and its bank notes in the 1940s and '50s. The explorer's deeds were documented in the country's social studies and history textbooks. And when the country adopted decimal currency in 1967, Cook's ship *Endeavour* was featured on the new fifty-cent piece. It still does, even though the coin is much reduced in size. In these various ways Cook has become immortalised throughout New Zealand.

This book will guide readers to the areas of special significance to James Cook's New Zealand, and place them firmly in their historical context.

THE EARLY LIFE OF JAMES COOK

James Cook was born in Marton, North Yorkshire, in 1728, the son of a Scottish farm labourer—also called James—and Grace Cook (nee Pace). When young James was eight years old the family moved to the village of Great Ayton, also in North Yorkshire, where his father obtained work at a nearby farm, Aireyholme. The second of eight children, James was raised in a two-room farm cottage in Great Ayton, locally called a 'biggin'.

James was taught to read and write in the village school, an education paid for by his father's employer, a Great Ayton landowner, Thomas Skottowe. During his four years at the school James proved a very able student, particularly in mathematics. He also worked on the Skottowe farm, assisting his father with his duties, before the landowner secured an apprenticeship for the young man with a merchant friend of his, William Sanderson.

Sanderson had a waterfront store at Staithes, a small port town on the Yorkshire coast, and at the age of sixteen James Cook moved to the town and began his apprenticeship in Sanderson's store. This employment lasted only eighteen months. Bored by shop work and fascinated by the nearby sea and the shipping movements he could see upon it, James decided that his future lay not upon the land but on the water. His life was about to take an entirely different course, one that would in time affect the history of the world.

In1746 eighteen-year-old James Cook abandoned his grocery apprenticeship and walked south to a larger Yorkshire port town, Whitby. There young James Cook trained as an apprentice merchant seaman under the tutelage of John Walker, a local ship owner and member of a prominent Whitby Quaker family.

Proving himself an adept student in all matters nautical, James first went to sea in 1747, aboard one of Walker's colliers, *Freelove*. For the next eight years Cook worked aboard other colliers, sailing north from Whitby to Tyneside to collect cargoes of coal, then south to the London docks, where the cargo was discharged. The east coast of England, with its reefs, shoals, currents and storms, made testing sailing, and in these waters James Cook was able to refine the skills he had learned in Walker's Whitby classroom.

In 1755 Cook made another life-changing decision. He turned his back on what had been a promising career as a merchant seaman and joined the Royal Navy. This meant starting all over again, first as an able seaman. After proving himself indeed able, in 1757 Cook was made a sailing Master. In the same year he saw active service against the French, with whom England was once again at war, on HMS *Eagle* and HMS *Pembroke*.

Later Cook proved to be a skilled hydrographer, carrying out outstanding work surveying the Gulf of St Lawrence, then the very complex coast of Newfoundland. He also successfully observed and recorded a solar eclipse, off the west coast of Newfoundland in 1766. These achievements confirmed Cook's exceptional abilities as an astronomer and coastal surveyor.

While staying in London in 1762 James met Elizabeth Batts, whom he married after a short courtship. A few months later he was appointed King's Surveyor, on the schooner HMS *Grenville,* and worked on her in Newfoundland, continuing to chart the island's coastline. In 1763, while he was working there, the first of James and Elizabeth's six children, a son James, was born. They were to have another four sons and a daughter, three of whom died in infancy.

In the mid-1760s Cook's astronomical, surveying and navigational abilities came to the attention of the influential Royal Society in London, as well as the British Admiralty. The 1769 transit of Venus was impending, and an expedition to the South Sea was mounted, to observe this important event on the far side of the

15

world. The commander of this challenging expedition would be of paramount importance.

In 1768 40-year-old James Cook was commissioned as a naval lieutenant and appointed to the command of HM Bark *Endeavour*, a selection supported by the Lords of the Admiralty. This inspired appointment eventually changed the map of the world.

The first of Cook's three world voyages began in Plymouth in August 1768 and ended in July 1771. It was during six months of those three years, and on subsequent voyages to the South Pacific, that the names 'James Cook' and 'New Zealand' became inextricably linked.

HM BARK *ENDEAVOUR*

The ship in which James Cook sailed to New Zealand, HM Bark *Endeavour*, was originally a collier, formerly called *The Earl of Pembroke*. Built at Fishburn's yard at Whitby, on England's north-east coast, she was three years, nine months old in 1768 and had been used to carry coal from Newcastle to London.

Endeavour has been described as 'a chunky little tub', designed and built to cope with the stormy conditions of the North Sea. The Lords of the Admiralty approved of the purchase of the collier for the sum of £2,840.10s.11d. Classed as a bark through the shape of her hull, she was refitted and renamed *Endeavour*. A square rigger of 374 tonnes, she was 30-metres long, about 9 metres wide and the height between her decks varied from 240 to 230 centimetres.

The Admiralty Lords and Cook were aware that the voyage to the 'South Sea' would make serious demands on the vessel. She would have to be capable of doubling Cape Horn as well as coping with tropical storms, coral-strewn waters and able to enter shallow tidal estuaries. Her holds needed ample space to accommodate the stores and provisions needed for a three-year voyage.

Endeavour was refitted at the naval yard at Deptford, London. Her bottom planks were sheathed with thin boards filled with large, flat-headed nails as protection against *teredo navalis*, a sea worm which bored into wood, especially in warm waters. To deal with any external threat, the ship had six carriage guns and twelve swivel guns. She had five anchors and carried a longboat, a pinnace and a yawl. The alterations to prepare her for her world voyage cost £11,798.17s.1d, a colossal sum in 1768.

Following his return to England in 1771, Cook did not sail in *Endeavour* again. She made three voyages to the Falkland Islands as a supply ship, but after that was sold off. Renamed the *Lord Sandwich,* she served as a troop transport during the War of American Independence. In August 1778 she was scuttled in Newport Harbour, Rhode Island, in an attempt to blockade the port against attacking American and French forces.

Since then the exact location of *Endeavour*'s remains have been unknown. But in May 2016 US archaeologists announced that they may have discovered the wreck of the vessel, in Newport Harbour. This find may mark the end of a lengthy debate about the final resting place of the ship commanded by Lieutenant James Cook during his first world circumnavigation.

THE *ENDEAVOUR* REPLICA

A replica of HM Bark *Endeavour* was built in Fremantle, West Australia, between 1988 and 1993. Owned by the Australian National Maritime Museum, the ship is based in Darling Harbour, Sydney. In 1995 the replica *Endeavour* recreated Cook's 1770 voyage along the east coast of Australia, then visited New Zealand. From late 1996 the replica circumnavigated the world, visiting ports in South Africa and the United Kingdom, including the first home port of the original *Endeavour*, Whitby.

The upper decks of the replica are as they were in the eighteenth century *Endeavour*. The crews sleep in hammocks slung from the deck head of the lower deck, as Cook's men did.

Although ostensibly a duplicate ship, the modern *Endeavour* carries equipment James Cook could never have dreamed of, modern devices that would have made a world of difference to his first circumnavigation of the globe. The replica has two Caterpillar 3046B diesel engines, providing 404 horsepower, located in what was the hold in the original *Endeavour*. Other twenty-first century technology on the replica include a desalinisation unit, modern bilge pumps, heads, showers and an electric galley. Modern communications and navigation equipment include a Global Positioning System.

A tour of the replica *Endeavour* provides a vivid impression of the cramped nature of the accommodation aboard an eighteenth century sailing ship, the complexity of its rigging and the demands this must have made upon its captain and crew.

Coastline near Gisborne

CHAPTER ONE

GISBORNE, POVERTY BAY & TOLAGA BAY

At 2pm saw land from the mast head bearing WBN, which we
stood directly for...

Gisborne city (population 36,100) is on the east coast of New Zealand's North Island. Its easterly location—longitude 178° 1' 4" East of Greenwich—gives it the distinction of being the first city in the world to see the light of a new day over the summer months. The city is located above a wide cove called Poverty Bay. Maori know the bay as Turanganui-a-Kiwa, which means 'Standing Place of Kiwa', and the larger East Coast region as Tairawhiti. The population of the Tairawhiti region is 41,000.

From the 1850s onwards the future site of Gisborne was home to just a few European traders and its Maori people, the tangata whenua. However in 1868 the New Zealand government bought land on the western bank of the Turanganui River and a proper town was founded. At first named Turanga, the name was changed to 'Gisborne' in honour of William Gisborne, New Zealand's then-colonial secretary. This happened in about 1880, because of confusion between Turanga and Tauranga, when Turanga's mail was being sent to Tauranga.

Behind Gisborne city is a wide, fertile plain built up by alluvial material brought down by rivers from mountains in the hinterland. The Turanganui River, which flows into Poverty Bay at its eastern end, is formed from the confluence of the Taruheru and Waimata rivers. The short Turanganui River then flows into Poverty Bay at the foot of Titirangi-Kaiti Hill, a headland to the south-east of the city. A stream, the Waikanae, flows into the Turanganui River from the west, near its estuary. The fine beach just to the west of the river mouth is also called Waikanae. Eastland Port, Gisborne, is an important centre for the export of pine logs. These are grown in plantations in the Eastland-Tairawhiti region, and then trucked to Gisborne for shipping to overseas markets, mainly in Asia.

A long golden sand beach, Te Oneroa, sweeps away to the south-west from the mouth of the Turanganui River. Poverty Bay, which fronts the beach, is broad and sheltered. 'Oneroa' means 'Long beach' and 'Waikanae', at its eastern end, means 'Waters of the yellow-eyed mullet'.

At the southern end of Poverty Bay a steep, white-cliffed headland extends out into the Pacific Ocean. This striking landmark is 'Young Nicks Head'; Maori know it as Te Kuri-a-Paoa.

The region's variety of excellent surf breaks and many fine ocean beaches, especially Wainui a few kilometres north-east of Gisborne, make the area a mecca for surfers.

The fertility of Poverty Bay's plain, combined with some of the highest sunshine hours in New Zealand—a yearly average of 2200 hours—mean that the region is noted for its horticulture, particularly citrus fruit, grapes, kiwifruit and squash. New Zealand's finest chardonnay wines are produced in Gisborne's wineries, along with other varieties such as viognier, gewurztraminer and chenin blanc.

Before the arrival of Europeans, the bay and its environs provided abundant food sources for the four main Maori tribes in the area. They were the descendants of people who arrived from the Polynesian homeland of Hawaiiki in the legendary voyaging canoes, Horouta and Takitimu. In 1769 the four tribes living around the bay were Rongowhakaata, Ngai Tahupoo, Te Aitanga-a-Mahaki and Te Aitanga-a-Hauiti. Each of these main tribes was divided into many hapu (sub-groups).

The rich soil and mild climate of Turanganui supported crops of taro, yams, kumara and fernroot. There was plentiful birdlife in the forests of kahikatea and tawa, there were eels and whitebait in the rivers and ducks on the lagoons. Crayfish and paua were plentiful in the rocky crevices around the shores below Titirangi-Kaiti, as well as extensive beds of pipi and mussels. In the bay Maori caught snapper, sharks, kahawai, kingfish and flounder. The tribes built their pa (fortified villages) on the bends of the rivers or on hilltop sites.

Gisborne and its surrounding districts today retain a strong Maori presence. Forty-eight per cent of the population identify as Maori, compared with the New Zealand average of 14.9 per cent. Two marae—Te Poho-o-Rawiri and Te Kuri a Tuatai—are located in the city's suburbs. The award-winning feature film, *Dark Horse* (2014), was based on the real-life story of a Maori man from Gisborne, Genesis Potini, a brilliant chess player who suffered from a severe bipolar disorder. The film had a strong Maori cast and was partly set in Potini's home city.

Poverty Bay's fertility and the past and present productivity of the region make the name given to it by James Cook highly ironic. However, placing the arrival and departure of Cook's *Endeavour* in its historical context explains how this singularly inapt name came about.

ENDEAVOUR'S VOYAGE: COOK'S FIRST LANDFALL

After the transit of Venus was observed in June 1769, *Endeavour* left Tahiti in August. Cook first took the ship south, to latitude 40°, in search of the Great Unknown Southern Continent. Having found no evidence of such a continent, he sailed back north, then west, towards the land Abel Tasman had first sighted on 13 December 1642.

Tasman's two ships had anchored three days later in Taitapu, a bay in the north-west of New Zealand's South Island. While attempting to go ashore in the ships' boats, several of Tasman's men were attacked and killed by local Maori. After naming the place 'Murderers' Bay' (today Golden Bay) Tasman sailed on up the west coast of the North Island. He named Cape Maria Van Diemen and the Three Kings Islands to the north of New Zealand, but made no further landings.

For the next 127 years there were no known European arrivals in the North or South Islands of what the Dutch had named 'Zeelandia Nova'—New Zealand. Until the sixth of October 1769, when the youngest person aboard *Endeavour*, Nicholas Young, the surgeon's servant boy, spied land from the masthead of *Endeavour*.

Having read translations of Tasman's journals, James Cook knew that the land young Nick had sighted must be the eastern coast of New Zealand.

After spending eight mostly cold weeks at sea, *Endeavour*'s company must have been highly excited at the prospect offered by the place that now lay before them. An entirely new land and people!

Cook recorded the scene as follows:

We saw in the Bay several Canoes, People upon the Shore, and some houses in the Country. The land on the Sea Coast is high, with Steep Cliffs; and back inland are very high Mountains. The face of the Country is of a hilly surface, and appears to be clothed with wood and Verdure.[1]

This typically understated Cook response to the arrival in New Zealand was not matched by that of *Endeavour*'s flamboyant naturalist, Joseph Banks. The sight of the mountains which formed the backdrop to the bay enthralled Banks. It suggested to him that they had come upon the great undiscovered continent, Terra Australis Incognita. Cook though, believed otherwise.

On 8 October *Endeavour* was worked into the bay at its eastern end, and its anchor lowered. The ship had been at sea for weeks, and Cook was keen to obtain much-needed food and water supplies. He was also anxious to establish relations with the local native people so that this could happen. He ordered the pinnace and yawl hoisted out and the two boats were rowed ashore and landed on the eastern bank of the Turanganui River. The landing party included a contingent of the ship's marines.

Cook ordered the pinnace to remain at the river mouth while the yawl took him, Lieutenant Gore and the civilians Banks, Solander, Monkhouse and Green upriver to look for the inhabitants of some houses they had seen in the area through their spyglasses. However they found that these dwellings had been abandoned.

As they were examining the house Cook's party heard a shot, coming from the place where the yawl had been left. A group of Maori had emerged from the nearby forest wielding spears, and were threatening the men guarding the boat. The Englishmen first fired warning shots, then when the warriors continued to advance, the pinnace's coxswain fired his musket and killed one of the warriors. His comrades first dragged the body a little way away, then left it on the river bank. The dead man was later identified as Te Maro, a member of the tribe that occupied the lands around the Titirangi headland.

This first meeting between Maori and Europeans had been fatal. But worse was to follow.

After hearing of the death, Cook ordered the boats to return to *Endeavour*. The following day they tried again. This time the longboat, as well as the pinnace and yawl, were rowed ashore. They carried a party of officers, the Raiatean priest-navigator Tupaia, the civilian scientists and armed marines, to the landing place on the eastern bank of the Turanganui River.

On the opposite river bank a group of armed warriors had assembled. They performed a ferocious haka, a ritual challenge to the strangers. With the aid of Tupaia, whose language the Maori understood, a tentative communication was established. One warrior swam across the river and landed on a large rock in the middle of the river. Cook waded over to greet him. The two men pressed noses. When more of the warriors crossed the river, Cook offered them beads and other trinkets in an attempt to show that they had come in peace. The warriors were indifferent to these gifts, however.

Instead they attempted to seize the Europeans' weapons. One snatched astronomer Green's short sword. Banks fired small shot into the back of the would-be thief, then Monkhouse fired a musket ball, fatally wounding him. The other warriors then retreated to the big rock in the middle of the river. After rallying there, they began to swim back towards Cook's men, clearly intending to attack. Cook, Green and Tupaia fired on them, wounding three with small shot, and one man mortally. This man's name was Te Rakau, and he was able to converse briefly with Tupaia before he died.

Having concluded that peaceful communication with these people was not possible, and because the water of the Turanganui River was brackish, Cook decided to seek an alternative landing place. *Endeavour*'s three boats were pulled further along the bay, towards the mouth of another river, the Kopututea.

As they did so they saw two canoes coming in from

the sea and heading towards the same river mouth. Tupaia called out a greeting to the men in one of the canoes but it began to paddle off rapidly. One of Cook's men fired a musket shot above the paddlers' heads and the canoe stopped. But when the pinnace came alongside the canoe its occupants attacked Cook's men, hurling stones and paddles and a bundle of fish at them. In retaliation the Endeavours fired upon the canoeists, killing four of them. Most of the others leapt overboard and swam ashore, but three boys who had been in the canoe were taken into the ship's boat and brought out to *Endeavour*.

Aboard the ship the boys, two brothers whose names were Te Haurangi and Ikirangi, and another called Marukauiti, were treated hospitably. They talked with Tupaia, asked and answered questions and even entertained their captors with a song and a dance. They relished the salt pork, bread and wine they were given by the crew.

This was the only bright light in what had otherwise been a grievous day. Both Cook and Banks recorded their deep regret at the earlier events. Banks wrote, 'Thus ended the most disagreeable day My life has yet seen…'[2]

A further landing was made the next morning, 10 October. The party walked along the bank of the Waikanae Stream, Banks and Solander collected botanical specimens and Cook shot some ducks. The three Maori boys accompanied the landing party, and with Tupaia acting as a mediator, peaceful contact was made with the uncle of Marukauiti, who had crossed the river bearing a green branch, a symbol of peace.

However a party of warriors had been seen assembling on the foreshore, suggesting that more hostilities could occur, so after giving the elderly man presents, Cook and his party, including the three boys, returned to *Endeavour*. To avoid further bloodshed Cook decided to sail on from the bay. The three boys were put ashore, where they rejoined their relatives, and when *Endeavour* sailed away the trio waved a poignant farewell from the beach.

To Cook's great disappointment, this first encounter with the natives of New Zealand had been a failure, producing almost nothing but misunderstandings and confrontation. Six Maori men had been killed. Furthermore, as a reprovisioning place the bay left much to be desired. Adequate supplies of fresh water, food and firewood had not been obtained and the naturalists had collected fewer than 40 new botanical specimens.

In his chagrin at what had occurred over the past three days, Cook named the place 'Poverty Bay', in his words, 'Because it afforded us no one thing we wanted.'

COMMEMORATING COOK IN GISBORNE

Although great changes have occurred in the Gisborne area, particularly over the last 100 years, the 1769 visit of Cook and *Endeavour* have not been forgotten. Fittingly, as the place of the explorer's first New Zealand landfall, there are more memorials to James Cook in Gisborne than any other place in New Zealand. His stay in Poverty Bay is commemorated in statuary and monument.

The geographical features that Cook recorded, notably Titirangi-Kaiti hill and the rivers which flow through the city, have not been obscured by twentieth and twenty-first century industrial developments.

For the visitor to Gisborne who wishes to see the places recorded in Cook's journal, these sites are located on both sides of the Turanganui River. They are not far apart and easily accessed by road or on foot.

An extension of Wainui Road/SH 35 becomes a bridge which crosses the Turanganui River. The road then turns sharply left and leads to a beachfront reserve where there is a statue of Cook and Nicholas Young, near the mouth of the Turanganui River, above Waikanae beach.

On the eastern side of the river, the Cook Landing Site National Historic Reserve is located on an area of reclaimed land beside the Esplanade Road, 1.4 kilometres down Kaiti Beach Road. The original shoreline is marked by a dip in the ground in front of the monument.

Unveiled on 8 October 1906, the Cook monument is an obelisk marking the approximate place where the explorer came ashore on 8 October 1769. The site is thus not far from the legendary rock islet in the river, which was called by Maori Te Toka-a-Taiau, where the first significant meeting between Maori and Europeans took place. This could have been New Zealand's equivalent of Plymouth Rock. Regrettably the sacred rock was blown up in 1877 as part of the development of Gisborne's harbour.

In 1990 the New Zealand Department of Conservation was given responsibility for the maintenance of the Cook Landing Site National Historic Reserve. Adding another dimension to the site, on the landward side of the obelisk is Banks Garden, in which grow representatives of some of the plants the botanist Joseph

Banks collected from the Tairawhiti region in 1769. Nearby Kaiti Beach, at the foot of Kaiti-Titirangi Hill, has an abundance of seabird life at low tide, particularly oyster catchers and stilts.

Kaiti-Titirangi Hill itself, which overlooks the port of Gisborne and mouth of the Turanganui River, provides fine views of the city, its agricultural hinterland, the long sweep of Te Oneroa beach and at the western end of Poverty Bay, Young Nicks Head-Te Kuri a Paoa.

There is a walking track up Kaiti-Titirangi Hill from the Cook monument. At the summit of the hill (135 metres), in Titirangi Drive, is the Cook Observatory, which is the 'World's Easternmost Observatory'. The Gisborne Astronomical Society meets here every Tuesday from 8.30pm (daylight saving time) and at 7.30pm (winter time).

Beside the road leading to the summit of Kaiti-Titirangi is Cook Plaza. Here there is a statue which purports to be a likeness of James Cook. It was donated by Captain Cook Breweries, of Auckland, to commemorate the James Cook bicentenary in 1969. Standing on a plinth, the statue is a bronze casting of a marble one, imported from Italy. It is modelled on an Italian admiral, and thus is not a true likeness of Cook.*

On the western bank of the Turanganui estuary is a Riverside Walkway, which follows the lower course of the river and crosses the Waikanae Creek to the beachfront reserve. Here, below the Waikanae Beach Holiday Park, is a far more authentic statue of Cook, a bronze by eminent sculptor Anthony Stones (1934–2016), erected in 1992.

The figure stands, legs firmly planted apart, on a semicircular marble base. The wording on the base reads:

A fine seaman, and outstanding captain and an honest man, Captain Cook was one of the last of the great explorer navigators and the first of the scientific expedition leaders. After his three global voyages of 1768–71, 1772–75 and 1776–79 the map of the world was substantially complete.

Here on the 9th and 10th of October, 1769, Cook walked with men from HM Bark Endeavour seeking fresh food and water. Nearby on the river rock Toka-a-Taiau, Maori chief and English greeted one another. When traditional challenges were misunderstood Maori were killed, the ship sailed without provisions and thus Poverty Bay received its name. From here, the Endeavour circumnavigated New Zealand and Cook plotted the first map of the country. This meeting of the two peoples marked the beginning of the New Zealand nation.

Etched into the globe base are the routes of James Cook's three world voyages.

Nearby, above Waikanae Beach, is another statue, one in bronze of Nicholas Young, *Endeavour*'s surgeon's boy, who first sighted New Zealand. 'Young Nick' is shown pointing not inland but out to sea, towards the dramatic, white-cliffed headland named after him, Young Nicks Head-Te Kuri a Paoa. The statue of the ship's boy was unveiled on 19 October 1969 by New Zealand's Governor General, Sir Arthur Porritt, as part of the Cook bicentenary celebrations.

The visitor to Gisborne should allow half a day to visit the above Cook-related sites. Recommended refreshment stops during the visit are a lunch or dinner at one of the several restaurants at the Gisborne Wharf, from where there are also views of the marina and the river. The wine should preferably be a Gisborne chardonnay.

A redevelopment of Gisborne's Inner Harbour is under way, a

joint venture between the local Council and the Eastland Group. This will provide for improved viewing of the river and the marina, better pedestrian access and connections and enhanced open space areas, with additional lighting and new plantings in the area. The development is due for completion by the end of 2018.

Another development of great significance to local iwi is a sculpture for placement alongside the mouth of the Turanganui River. Entitled *Hawaiki Turanga,* the sculpture acknowledges the historical importance of this site by honouring the arrival of waka, which brought the ancestors from whom the iwi of Turanganui a Kiwa are descended. The design of *Hawaiki Turanga* is by artist-engineer Matt Randall, who has tribal affiliations with the local hapu.

To summarise Gisborne's various Cook's memorials:

- ঌ Statues of Cook and Nicholas Young beside the Turanganui river mouth

- ঌ Cook Landing Site National Historic Reserve, Kaiti Beach Road

- ঌ Cook monument obelisk, Kaiti Beach Road

- ঌ Joseph Banks Garden. Kaiti Beach Road

- ঌ Cook Observatory, Titirangi Drive

- ঌ Cook Plaza statue, Kaiti-Titirangi Hill

*Nevertheless, the fact that the statue was donated by a brewery is not entirely irrelevant. Cook's men were the first to brew beer in New Zealand, in Dusky Sound, in 1773. (See the chapter on Dusky Sound.)

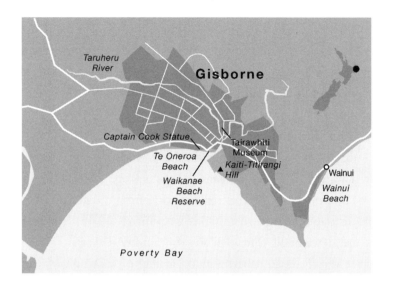

Map of Gisborne

The Oneroa beachfront cycle & walkway

The one-kilometre-long Oneroa beachfront cycle and walkway extends along the Waikanae foreshore, behind the beach's sand dunes and under the shade of a row of mature Norfolk pine trees. The raised boardwalk and concrete link tells the story of the Waikanae district, while providing unimpeded views of the sea. Cultural elements incorporated in the overall design were contributed by a local artist, Derek Lardelli.

The Gisborne i-SITE Visitor Information Centre is located on the bank of the Waikanae Creek, at 209 Grey Street. Phone (06) 868 6139. The creek is the one on which Cook shot ducks, on 10 October 1769.

Websites: www.outeast.co.nz; www.gisbornenz.com

The Tairawhiti museum and art gallery

This museum and art gallery features a variety of changing and semipermanent exhibitions pertaining to the Tairawhiti-Gisborne region. It contains numerous displays of East Coast Maori and colonial history. Located near the banks of the Taruheru River in Gisborne, the museum is at Kelvin Rise, Stout Street, Gisborne. Its calendar of exhibitions can be viewed at www.tairawhitimuseum.org.nz.
Email: info@tairawhitimuseum.org.nz.

ENDEAVOUR'S VOYAGE: SAILING SOUTH

After weighing anchor in Poverty Bay, Cook took *Endeavour* south along the North Island's east coast. Again, this was in accordance with the Admiralty's instructions to take the ship to 40° South latitude whenever possible.

While sailing along this coast *Endeavour* was met by several large canoes with ornately carved prows. Some of their occupants came aboard and traded peacefully; others were hostile, surrounding the ship and making threatening gestures. Whenever such threats were issued, Cook ordered muskets or cannons fired over the aggressors' heads. This dramatic display of firepower usually caused the canoes to be paddled off rapidly.

A large bay at 39° South latitude Cook named 'Hawke Bay', after Sir Edward Hawke, First Lord of the Admiralty. At the southern end of this bay is a prominent headland. On 15 October 1769, Maori traders in canoes surrounded *Endeavour*, exchanging fish for Tahitian bark cloth. Taiata, Tupaia's Tahitian servant boy, was assisting with the trading, handing up fish to the ship. As he did so some of the Maori in the canoes seized him and began to paddle off, possibly thinking the boy was being held on *Endeavour* against his will. The marines aboard the ship were ordered to fire muskets at the would-be kidnappers, and two or three of them were killed.

In the ensuing confusion Taiata jumped from the canoe and swam back to *Endeavour*. This incident prompted Cook to name the nearby headland 'Cape Kidnappers'.

The following day *Endeavour* reached latitude 40° 34' South. As no harbour could be seen and no fresh water could be obtained, Cook ordered the ship to be put about. His instructions having been fulfilled, they would now revert to a northerly course and survey the remaining sections of the North Island's east coast.

This time *Endeavour* bypassed Poverty Bay.

CAPE KIDNAPPERS

Today Cape Kidnappers is renowned for being one of only two places on the New Zealand mainland which provide a nesting ground for the Australasian gannet, *Morus serrator*, whose Maori name is takapu. The other New Zealand mainland breeding site is at Muriwai, on Auckland's west coast. The Cape Kidnappers colony is the largest in the world. There are about 6500 breeding pairs of the birds and their sanctuary is sited spectacularly, 100 metres above the Pacific Ocean.

The Australasian gannet has a 1.8-metre wingspan. Its body is slender, with white plumage, a buff-yellow head and neck, and blue skin around its eyes. The birds are plunge divers, hurtling vertically from a great height into the sea to catch squid or pelagic fish such as pilchards.

The gannets usually arrive at Cape Kidnappers in late July. In October and November their eggs are laid and take about six weeks to hatch. The best time to see the birds is thus between early November and late February. By March they begin to emigrate and by April they are almost all gone. From June to October the sanctuary is closed.

Several tour operators take visitors to the Cape Kidnappers breeding colony, either along the beach from Clifton, the last settlement on the coast before the cape, on a tractor-pulled trailer, or overland on 4WD vehicles. It is also possible to take the ten-kilometre walk from Clifton, but if doing so tide times must be taken into consideration.

The Cape Kidnappers tide schedule is available from the Napier i-SITE, Marine Parade, Napier. Phone 0800 84 74 88 or 06 834 1911; Email: info@napiernz.com; Website: www.napiernz.com.

For further information about the gannet colony see www.hawkesbaynz.com/index.php/why/go-gannets.

TOLAGA BAY

Tolaga, sometimes known as Uawa, is the name of both a bay and a small town on New Zealand's East Coast, 45 kilometres north-east of Gisborne. The bay is enclosed by rugged hills and protected by headlands to the north and south. Some Maori people of the district refer to the area as Hauiti and Tolaga town is the base of the Te Aitanga-a-Hauiti iwi.

Tolaga Bay is drained by the Uawa River, which flows into the ocean near the centre of the bay. There is a bar at the mouth of the river and an island, Pourewa, just off the headland at the bay's southern end.

Because Tolaga Bay is shallow, a 600-metre-long wharf—the longest in the Southern Hemisphere—was built in the 1920s, to allow ships to collect agricultural commodities such as wool from the farmland in the bay's hinterland. The wharf no longer has this function; the last cargo of maize was shipped from it in 1967, and for a time it was threatened with demolition, but a campaign was mounted to restore it and the refurbishment is now complete. The long wharf is popular with fishermen and visitors to the bay.

Tolaga township is located on a plain between the Uawa River and the bay. Laid out in a grid pattern, many of the town's streets are named after Cook's men and his ships. There is a Banks Street, Monkhouse Street, Solander Street, Parkinson Street, Furneaux Street, Endeavour Street, Resolution Street, Discovery Street and Adventure Street.

Why all these Cook-related names In Tolaga town? Because for one week in 1769, from 22 to 29 October, Cook's *Endeavour* was anchored in the bay and his company was made welcome ashore. Four years later, in October 1773, Tobias Furneaux and his ship HMS *Adventure* also found sanctuary in the bay, after being driven north by a gale off the south-east coast of the North Island. For the second time, *Adventure* had become separated from Cook's *Resolution,* during his second world voyage.

When *Endeavour* reached Anaura Bay, a few miles north of Tolaga Bay, on 21 October 1769, her company was sorely in need of provisions. Poverty Bay had afforded them almost no provisions. *Endeavour*'s company did obtain some fresh water from Anaura Bay, but heavy surf prevented a full-scale landing. Informed that there was a more sheltered bay a little further to the south, Cook took *Endeavour* back down the coast and anchored her a mile off-shore from Tolaga Bay's southern headland. Hoping that this area would supply them with the water, food and wood they so badly needed, Cook decided to stay in the bay for some days.

Just around the headland at the southern end of Tolaga Bay was a sheltered inlet, called by the local Maori Opoutama. It is known today as Cook's Cove. The area surrounding it was well-wooded and a stream, the Turanui, flowed into the cove. The local people, the Te Aitanga-a-Hauiti descent group, were friendly and welcoming. The ship's naturalists, Banks, Solander and Sporing, were delighted with the many new plant specimens that grew around the bay. Botanical illustrator Sydney Parkinson drew the specimens beautifully and made sketches of the coastal landforms.

In all respects, Tolaga Bay was everything that Poverty Bay had not been. The large population was prosperous and peaceful, its rich alluvial soil was well cultivated with extensive plantations of kumara and yams. The people's canoes and houses were embellished with ornate carvings and the settlement included an esteemed house of learning, called Te Rawheoro. Crayfish were plentiful in the bay, along with shellfish, kahawai and hapuka. At the end of their first day in the cove, twelve tonnes of water and three boatloads of wood were taken out to *Endeavour*. Parkinson drew a sketch of the watering party working at the place where the Turanui Stream flowed into Cooks Cove, and wrote a lyrical description of its beauty.

A few hundred yards from the beach the visitors found a 'noble arch'; a hole through the face of a rock leading directly to the sea, with a stream running through it. This spectacular landform the Maori called metaphorically 'Te Kotore o te Whenua', meaning 'The

Anus of the land'. Banks extolled this natural feature, writing, 'It was certainly the most magnificent surprise I have ever met with so much is pure nature superior to art in these cases.'[2]

Tupaia, the high-born priest-navigator from Raiatea, who was aboard *Endeavour*, was treated with great deference by the people of Tolaga Bay. He spent most of the week ashore, conversing with the chiefs and priests and exchanging stories of their common Polynesian tupuna (ancestors).

No doubt delighted that peaceful and meaningful communication had at last been established with some of the New Zealanders, and with *Endeavour* fully provisioned and her company refreshed, on 29 October Cook ordered her anchors weighed. The Tolaga Bay-Uawa stopover had been everything Cook hoped it would, but there was much more uncharted coastline of this new land to survey.

TOLAGA BAY AND COOK'S COVE TODAY

Tolaga Bay is a popular holiday centre. Near the wharf there is a holiday park, and in the township there is an inn, a lodge and several motels. Walking the town's streets, their names are a constant reminder of the positive meetings between Tolaga Bay Maori and Cook's men, nearly 250 years ago.

Another reminder of that provenance is the Cooks Cove Walkway. This track is 5.8 kilometres long and returns via the same route. Walking time is 2 hours 30 minutes. It requires medium levels of fitness, as some hill climbing is involved. Suitable walking shoes are recommended.

Also note that the track is closed from 1 August until the beginning of Labour Weekend, in late October. This is because

Tairawhiti-Eastland is sheep farming country and from August until late October is the region's lambing season.

From SH 35, take the Wharf Road turn-off, which is two kilometres south of Tolaga Bay township. The track begins at the southern end of the bay. There is a small car park adjacent to the walkway entrance, and a larger one at the beach car park, adjacent to the motor camp, 200 metres beyond the beginning of the track.

The first stage of the track crosses a small paddock. It then climbs through light bush and across open grassland, keeping to a farm track just above the tops of the cliffs. Twenty minutes further on there is a lookout point, 120 metres above the sea. The lookout provides the first views of Cooks Cove. A cluster of islets—Mitre Rocks—rise to the left of the entrance to the inlet, while on the right is Pourewa Island.

The track then winds down through regenerating forest, and 200 metres later passes a small pond before coming to the cove's coastal lowland. Here there is a memorial commemorating Cook's 1769 visit, erected by the New Zealand Historic Places Trust in 1966. From here too can be viewed the striking hole in the rock wall, Te Kotere o te Whenua.

A case can be made for this cove being the site of one of the most positive meeting places between *Endeavour*'s men and New Zealand Maori during Cook's first world voyage.

A picnic lunch at Cook Cove before the return walk is highly recommended.

Website: www.doc.govt.nz/parks-and-recreation/places-to-go/east-coast/places/tolaga-bay-area/

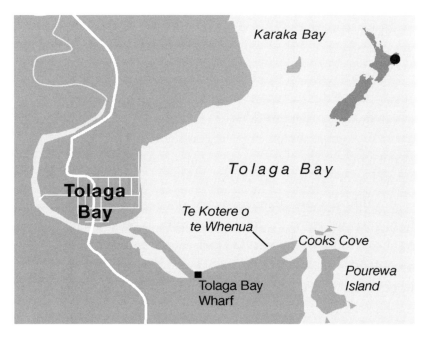

Map of Tolaga Bay

Young Nick's Head from Gisborne

The Whale Rider

South of Tolaga Bay, branching off SH 35, is the small settlement of Whangara. This is the setting for the novel *The Whale Rider* (1987), by the noted New Zealand Maori writer, Witi Ihimaera, whose family is from the East Coast. The novel provides insights into local Maori culture and mythology, and as such makes informative background reading to the East Coast region. In 2002 *The Whale Rider* was made into a feature film, starring Keisha Castle-Hughes as the main character, the 12-year-old Maori girl, Pai, who aspires to be a chieftainess of her tribe.

ANOTHER TRANSIT OF VENUS

It was to observe a transit of the planet Venus across the face of the sun, on 6 June 1769, that brought James Cook across the world to Tahiti.

Transits of Venus occur in pairs, eight years apart, with over a century between the pairs. They occur in June and December of the transit years. Following the 1761 and 1769 transits, the next pair occurred in 1874 and 1882.

There were transits of Venus again in 2004 and 2012. The 8 June 2004 transit was not visible from New Zealand, but astronomers were aware that the one on 6 June 2012 would be. Accordingly, given Cook's strong connection with the place, the authorities considered it fitting that Tolaga Bay would be the best location for the official observation of the 6 June 2012 transit.

The 2012 Transit of Venus Project was a partnership between Te Aitanga a Hauiti and the Tolaga Bay community, the MacDiarmid Institute, the Royal Society of New Zealand, Victoria University of Wellington and the Allan Wilson Centre, Massey University. On

6 June a crowd assembled at the bay to observe the rare cosmic phenomenon. Most watched from the very long Tolaga Bay wharf, which provided a fine grandstand for the observation.

The weather was cloudy throughout most of New Zealand, obscuring the sun and making an observation difficult. However at Tolaga Bay, during the singing of the New Zealand national anthem, almost miraculously the sky cleared. Journalist Toby Manhire described this phenomenon as, 'A magical day on the east coast, as the sun shines, and Venus slides across it.'

Many people had assembled on the wharf and beach to view the steady progress of the black dot of Venus moving across the face of the sun. They gazed upwards, watching the special sight with cardboard sunglasses.

The Tolaga Bay observation was a great success. Later, a Transit of Venus Forum was held in Gisborne, 750 trees were planted at the mouth of the Uawa River and there was a dramatised re-enactment of Cook's 1769 landing at the bay, performed by students of the Tolaga Bay Area School. It was a true community celebration.

There will not be another pair of transits of Venus until June and December 2117 and June and December 2125.

ANAURA BAY

Seventeen kilometres north from Tolaga Bay on SH 35, a road branches off to the right. At the end of this seven-kilometre-long road is Anaura Bay, where Cook's *Endeavour* lowered her anchors on 21 October 1769.

Maori came out in canoes to greet the ship. Two elderly chiefs came aboard and gifts were exchanged. Cook and others, including the civilian naturalists, then went ashore at the southern end of

Anaura Bay in the ship's boats, hoping to obtain fresh water from two streams that flowed into the bay. However a strong wind blew up, creating wild surf that made it difficult to get the water casks back to the ship. The Maori offered to transfer the party back to *Endeavour* in one of their canoes, but it was swamped by the surf, obliging the visitors to spend some time ashore. There they were received hospitably, no doubt to their relief after the earlier violent confrontations at Turanganui.

Anaura Bay was home to a tribal community of about 150 people. Banks and the other naturalists 'botanised' and were impressed by the carefully tended garden plots on the hill slopes, which were planted in kumara, taro and yams. Herman Sporing sketched the surrounding hills and gardens and officer Richard Pickersgill drew a plan of the bay. *Endeavour*'s water casks were filled and wood supplies were cut. The visitors referred to the bay as 'Tegadoo', probably a misinterpretation of the Maori name, 'Te Karu'.

The Anaura Bay people also provided the visitors with some important information: there was a more sheltered bay a little further to the south, called Uawa, or Tolaga Bay. After the visitors returned to *Endeavour* Cook ordered the ship's anchors weighed. *Endeavour* then backtracked just over five nautical miles south to more sheltered Uawa-Tolaga Bay and there the company spent a productive week ashore.

Anaura Bay is one of the loveliest bays on the East Coast of the North Island. It is surrounded by steep hills which slope down to a level foreshore. The bay has a white sand beach, sheltered by a headland to the north and by Motuoroi Island in the south. Also at its southern end is the Anaura marae. Descendants of a famous Maori chief, Hauiti, lived in the Anaura Bay district, and the marae's meeting house, Hinetamatea, is named after a member of Hauiti's family.

A plaque at the southern end of Anaura Bay marks the place where the *Endeavour* party came ashore on 21 October, 1769.

There are scenic reserves on the foreshore of Anaura Bay, and a campsite at its northern end. Numerous baches and holiday accommodation at the bay are available for rental.

Websites: www.doc.govt.nz/anaurabaycampsite; www.holidayhouses.co.nz/Anaura-Bay.asp.

Lonely Bay and Cooks Beach from Shakespeare Cliff

CHAPTER TWO

EAST COAST & THE BAY OF PLENTY

This point of land I have called East Cape, because I have great reason to think that it is the Eastern-most land on this whole Coast.

ENDEAVOUR'S VOYAGE—EAST CAPE

East Cape is the easternmost point of the main islands of New Zealand. Its coordinates are 37° 69' South latitude and 178° 54' East longitude. A small island, East Island, lies off the cape, which is known as Whangaokeno by Maori. The majority of the population of the East Coast region is Maori and is steeped in traditional mythology.

Cook made no landings here. He was aware of the need to sail on, knowing that a transit of Mercury would occur on 9 November and that they must therefore find a suitable location from which to observe it.

James Cook and *Endeavour* doubled East Cape on 30 October 1769.

East Cape is reached by a secondary road which leads off SH 35 from the tiny settlement of Te Araroa. In the grounds of the township's school stands an ancient pohutukawa tree. Called Te Waha-o-Rerekohu, it is said to be about 600 years old, meaning that the tree was already old when Cook sailed past in 1769.

From Te Araroa the road clings to the coast and after 22 kilometre comes to an end at the mouth of a small stream. Above the cape is Otiki Hill (154 metres). There is a fully automated lighthouse on the hill. The area around the lighthouse is accessible on foot up a series of steps, but the house itself is not open to the public. From the hill there are delightful views of the coast around East Cape and out to East Island.

Returning to SH 35, the highway goes directly west and past Hicks Bay, one of the loveliest beaches in Eastland. The bay was named by Cook in honour of Zachary Hicks (1739?–1771), who was a lieutenant on *Endeavour,* and Cook's second-in-command. Hicks died of tuberculosis on the voyage back to England.

Cape Runaway, on the western side of East Cape, is so-named because when several Maori canoes approached *Endeavour* while she was rounding the cape and showed signs of aggression towards the ship and its company, Cook ordered the cannons fired over the heads of the canoeists. The detonations alarmed their occupants into hastily 'running' away from the ship.

Mount Hikurangi

Mt Hikurangi (1752 metres) is in the Raukumara Range, 50 kilometres south-west of the East Cape lighthouse and 80 kilometres north of Gisborne. The mountain lies within the rohe (tribal area) of the Ngati Porou tribe.

In Maori mythology Hikurangi is said to be the first part of the North Island—Te Ika a Maui—that emerged when the legendary Polynesian hero Maui pulled the island from the ocean as a giant fish. Maui's waka (canoe), called Nukutaimemeha, was stranded on the mountain and became petrified near its summit. Hikurangi's peak is said to be the first land on Earth to catch the rays of the new day's sun.

It is likely that Cook and his men would have seen Mount Hikurangi from the decks of *Endeavour* as they sailed along the East Coast in October 1769.

THE BAY OF PLENTY & WHITE ISLAND

During the first week of November 1769, Cook sailed across a broad bay. *Endeavour* made no landing on its shores, but through their telescopes Cook and his officers observed a wide plain. The land appeared very fertile. It was extensively cultivated, densely populated, and there was a series of palisaded villages on the coastal cliff-tops. A volcanic cone protruding from the plain Cook named 'Mt Edgecumbe'. Today it is called Putauaki (821 metres), but Edgecumbe town, north-west of the mountain on SH 2, retains Cook's name.

In view of the area's obvious prosperity, Cook named it 'The Bay of Plenty'. Confirming Cook's impression, today this fertile, high sunshine area is New Zealand's premium horticultural region, noted in particular for its kiwifruit, avocado and citrus orchards. The Bay of Plenty's principal urban centre, Tauranga (135,000), is New Zealand's fifth largest and fastest growing city.

While traversing the Bay of Plenty those aboard *Endeavour* also observed, about 40 kilometres to the south-east, an island shrouded in white steam. Accordingly, Cook named it 'White Island'. Maori knew it as Whakaari, meaning 'the Dramatic Volcano'.

White Island is New Zealand's most continuously active marine volcano. Forty-eight kilometres from the East Coast, the island has been built up by volcanic activity over the past 150,000 years and marks the north-eastern extent of the Taupo Volcanic Zone. Within this zone are areas of intense volcanic activity, including geysers, mud pools and dormant volcanoes.

White Island is roughly circular and about two kilometres in diameter. It rises to 321 metres above sea level. During the last decades of the nineteenth century and the early years of the twentieth, there was a sulphur mine on the island. It was abandoned in September 1914, after part of the island's western crater rim collapsed, creating a laha, or mud-flow, which killed all ten mine workers.

Volcanic activity today on White Island consists mostly of steaming fumaroles and boiling mud pools. However, in March 2000 three vents appeared in the main crater and began emitting fine grey ash, which covered the island. Later in the same year an eruption covered it in mud and scoria and a new crater appeared. These events underscored the fact that a major eruption of the island could occur at any time. Temperatures of 600° to 800° Celsius have been recorded on the island's crater floor.

Volcanologists continually monitor White Island with seismographic equipment, since an explosive eruption would likely trigger a tsunami that could inundate the nearest coastal towns, Opotiki, Whakatane and Tauranga-Mt Maunganui. Hence, all along the Bay of Plenty coast there are tsunami warning signs and instructions for mass evacuations should one occur.

For those wishing to see inside White Island, an all-day tour by boat can be taken to the island when sea conditions permit, or helicopter flights can be taken over it.

White Island Tours: 15 the Strand, Whakatane.

Phone: (07) 308 9588.

A wreck on Astrolabe Reef

The Bay of Plenty was the site of New Zealand's worst environmental calamity, an event which began in the early morning of 5 October 2011, when a container ship went aground on Astrolabe Reef.

Astrolabe Reef is close to Motiti Island, off the Bay of Plenty coast. The reef, which breaks the water at low tide, is a favourite site for scuba divers, dropping off to 37 metres in various parts. The reef was named by the French navigator Jules Dumont d'Urville, for his vessel *Astrolabe*, after it almost went aground on the rocks on 16 February 1827. Evidently James Cook either avoided the reef or a high tide covered it, when he sailed *Endeavour* past it, early in November 1769, 58 years before d'Urville's near-mishap.

On Wednesday 5 October 2011, the container ship MV *Rena* was sailing from Napier to the port of Tauranga. Liberian-registered, she was 236 metres in length, had a gross tonnage of 39,410 and carried a crew of twenty. *Rena* was owned by the Greek shipping company Costamare Inc. through a subsidiary, Daina Shipping and had been built in 1990.

At 2.20am on 5 October the ship's master took a short cut from the proper passage, to save time for his vessel's arrival in Tauranga. *Rena* struck Astrolabe Reef at full speed and was impaled upon it.

A few days later, after *Rena*'s crew had been evacuated, oil began washing ashore on the Bay of Plenty coastline, including on Mt Maunganui beach, one of the bay's loveliest. A five-kilometre-long oil slick threatened sea birdlife and the bay's rich fishing waters. Volunteers worked to clean up the beaches and rescue and clean seabirds fouled by the oil slick.

On 11 October the spill was officially declared to be New Zealand's worst ever environmental disaster. The following week, rocked by the waves, *Rena* had begun to list. Many of the ship's containers, some holding toxic chemicals, fell into the sea. Several washed ashore on pristine beaches. A few months later, during stormy weather, the vessel broke in two. By 10 January *Rena*'s stern section had almost completely sunk.

In 2012 the *Rena*'s owners were fined $300,000 in the Tauranga District Court after pleading guilty to a charge under New Zealand's *Resource Management Act*, relating to the discharge of harmful substances following the grounding.

By 2014 the wreck had been salvaged of three-quarters of the containers and major pieces of the superstructure removed, as well as all the fuel and oils.

By 2016 the wreck of the *Rena* was deemed to no longer present a hazard to shipping. In April of that year the four-and-a-half-year exclusion zone around the *Rena* was lifted and the reef opened once again for recreational diving and fishing. The wreck has now become part of the reef's marine ecosystem and is an advanced dive site in two areas.

A final report into the causes and circumstances of the

grounding found that it was the failure of the master and crew to follow proper voyage planning, navigation and watch-keeping practices, and the managers' insufficient oversight of *Rena*'s safety management system that led to the grounding.

Lieutenant James Cook RN would have been singularly unimpressed.

Website: www.taurangafishingcharters.co.nz/diving-trips/
Website: www.taurangadive.co.nz

MAYOR ISLAND

On 3 November 1769, still sailing across the Bay of Plenty, those aboard *Endeavour* sighted another large island. In view of the fact that Lord Mayor's Day would be celebrated shortly on the other side of the world in London, Cook named it 'Mayor Island'.

Maori called this island 'Tuhua'. It was very important to them as a source of black obsidian, volcanic glass created by the rapid cooling of silica-rich lava. Tuhua's obsidian was highly valued as a cutting tool and as such was traded for other precious commodities such as greenstone throughout much of New Zealand. The island was the ancestral home of the Whanau A Tauwhao Ki Tuhua people. Today it is privately owned and administered by the Tuhua Trust Board.

Mayor Island is a dormant shield volcano 35 kilometres north of the city of Tauranga. Thirteen square kilometres in area, it rises to 355 metres above sea level. There are two small crater lakes, Green Lake and Black Lake, on the island, and many hot springs. Its most recent lava flows have been dated at between 500 and 1000 years. Bush-covered, the island is a wildlife refuge where native birds such as the tui, bellbird, wood pigeon, kaka and grey warbler thrive.

The waters around Mayor Island are famous for game fishing. Swordfish, marlin and mako sharks are taken in the vicinity, although the waters close to the island are a marine reserve.

Mayor Island is very popular with recreationalists such as scuba divers, trampers and ornithologists. To protect the island's wildlife against invasive predators such as mice and rats, biosecurity checks are made of all visitors, to ensure that such creatures do not gain access to the island.

Fishing charters and day tours to Mayor Island can be taken from Whakatane or Tauranga. The tours are weather-dependent. The vessel *Moutohora Cat* sails to the island from Whakatane and the vessel *Enterprise* sails there from Tauranga.

Refer to Seatrek Marine Charter Company, J Pier, Sulphur Point marina, Tauranga City. Phone: 0274 969 973; 0508 GOSEATREK.

THE ALDERMEN ISLANDS

Making one of his rare forays into metaphor, the same day that he named Tuhua 'Mayor Island', James Cook called a cluster of islets further north 'The Court of Aldermen'. They are known today as the Aldermen Islands.

The Aldermens are on the eastern Coromandel coast, twenty kilometres east of the Tairua River mouth, at 36° 58' South and 176° 05' East. The remnants of an exploded volcanic cone, the group comprises four main islands: Hongiora, Middle, Ruamahuanui and Ruamahuaiti. Their combined land area is just under one square kilometre. The Aldermens are a forested nature reserve where rare native species, including tuatara, live. Although landing on the islands is only allowed by permit, the waters around the Aldermens are popular with scuba divers.

On clear days both Mayor Island and the Aldermens can be seen from the numerous high vantage points along SH 25, such as the lookout on the hill five kilometres north of Tairua town. The rugged islands make a fine spectacle.

The Pacific Coast Highway

The Pacific Coast Highway incorporates a large area of the upper part of New Zealand's North Island. The route passes through some of the country's most scenic coastal landscapes.

Following the Pacific Ocean's coastline for most of its route, the one-way highway is about 1027 kilometres long. It begins either in Auckland (driving clockwise) or Hastings (anticlockwise) and ends in either Hastings or Auckland.

The highway is signposted throughout its length and passes several of the districts which James Cook saw and named during his 1769-70 circumnavigation of New Zealand. These areas include the Firth of Thames, the Coromandel Peninsula, the Bay of Plenty, Eastland and Hawkes Bay.

Driving the Pacific Coast Highway in its entirety takes a minimum of four days.

For a detailed itinerary of the Pacific Coast Highway route, refer to the website: pacificcoasthighwayguide.co.nz.

Beginning of the Cathedral Cove walkway

CHAPTER THREE

THE COROMANDEL

I took formal possession of the place in the Name of His Majesty...

ENDEAVOUR'S VOYAGE: THE COROMANDEL PENINSULA AND THE TRANSIT OF MERCURY

Mercury Bay, on the eastern Coromandel coast, is known to its Maori people as 'Te-Whanganui-a-Hei', which means 'The Great Bay of Hei'. Hei was an important ancestor of the local Maori tribe, the Ngati Hei. The township of Hahei, a popular holiday settlement on the coast, is also named after this chief.

James Cook and *Endeavour* sailed into the Great Bay of Hei on the evening of 4 November 1769. The ship was greeted by canoes occupied by people from the Ngati Hei tribe, who welcomed the strange visitors to their shores.

Endeavour's company spent twelve days in the bay and surrounding area. The expedition's main purpose was to observe a transit of Mercury across the face of the sun, an event which is far more common than a transit of Venus. Transits of Mercury occur thirteen times every century, since Mercury is far closer to the sun than Venus. Nevertheless, astronomers were keen for the Mercury transit to be closely observed and recorded, as this could also help establish the precise distance between the Earth and the Sun. This in turn could help establish the exact calculation of longitude.

Cook also wished to obtain fresh food and firewood supplies while in the bay, fill *Endeavour*'s water casks, and heel and scrub the ship's hull.

Cook wrote of their stay in the bay he called 'Mercury':

Wednesday 8ᵗʰ November, 1769 pm

Fresh breeze at NNW and hazey rainy weather, the remainder a gentle breeze at WSW and Clear weather. AM heel'd and scrubed both sides of the Ship and sent a party of men a Shore to cut wood and fill water. The Natives brought to the ship and sold us for small pieces of Cloth as much fish as served all hands, they were of the Mackerel kind and as good as ever was eat.[1]

An observatory was set up on the shore, about 100 metres west of the Purangi River mouth. There, on 9 November, in fine, clear spring weather, Cook and his astronomer Charles Green successfully observed the transit of Mercury. The coordinates of the site were recorded by the pair as 36° 50' South latitude and 175° 45' East longitude. Contemporary coordinates of the site are stated as 36° 47' and 175° 48'. These minor variations from Cook and

Green's 1769 recordings are an indication of the skill and care of their calculations.

The Purangi River, named by Cook 'Oyster Brook', after its quantities of shellfish beds, flows into the bay where the transit was observed, at its eastern end. The inner part of the bay is 'Cook's Bay' and the headland above the river mouth 'Cook Bluff'. A three-kilometre-long, golden sand shore fronts the bay, and is called 'Cook's Beach'. A cluster of islands 25 kilometres north of the bay were named the 'Mercury Islands'.

THE COROMANDEL PENINSULA

The Coromandel Peninsula projects from the north-eastern coast of the North Island. According to Maori legend, the first discoverers of the Coromandel were voyagers from East Polynesia, and so somewhere on the east coast of the peninsula may well have been the site of the first arrival of human beings in New Zealand. Maori tradition also has it that these first arrivals were led by the great Polynesian navigator, Kupe. The time of their arrival of these ocean voyagers on the peninsula is debatable, but is thought to have been about 1300 AD.[2]

Today the Coromandel Peninsula is a popular holiday destination, two hours' drive from Auckland city. During the summer months the peninsula is crowded with holidaymakers. Native pohutukawa trees (*Metrosideros excels*) grow along the coastline and bloom brilliantly crimson at Christmas time. The coastline on the eastern side of the peninsula is particularly suitable for boating, camping, swimming, surfing and recreational fishing.

The best-known Coromandel holiday locations are Pauanui,

Tairua, Hot Water Beach, Hahei, Cathedral Cove, Cook's Beach, Whitianga, Opito Bay, Matarangi, Whangapoua and adjoining New Chums beach. All these are on the east coast of the peninsula, which *Endeavour* sailed past in late 1769.

Cook's Beach is near the end of the Purangi Road, which branches right from SH 25 at Whenuakite. The Cook's Beach settlement consists mainly of holiday houses and subdivisions, built on a level foreshore lowland. The Cook's Beach shopping centre is in Captain Cook Road, a couple of streets back from the beach. Other streets in the settlement which commemorate *Endeavour*'s 1769 visit include Banks Street and Charles Green Drive.

The site where the transit of Mercury was observed in 1769 is on Captain Cook Road, near the eastern end of the beach. Here a sign and concrete cairn denote the observation site.

The Purangi River flows into the sea a little to the east of the cairn. About 200 metres above the river mouth a stream rises in the hills behind Cook Bluff, then flows down a narrow valley. It was from this unnamed stream that *Endeavour*'s water casks were filled during the ship's stay in the bay, gravity assisting the watering party's work.

On 14 November 1769, on a knoll above the stream, James Cook 'took formal possession of the place' for Britain and raised the 'King's Colours'. An inscription was cut into a tree trunk, stating the date and the name of *Endeavour*.

This event occurred six weeks after Cook's arrival in New Zealand. It is thought that he allowed the claim to be delayed because he wanted to ensure that he kept accordance with his 'Instructions' from the British Admiralty that he should not formally claim the new land for Britain until he had obtained 'the Consent of the Natives'. Although no formal consent had been received from the Maori people, who in any event could not be expected to speak for the whole population of New Zealand, Cook's generally friendly relations with the people of Anaura and Tolaga Bays, then Mercury Bay, allowed Cook to believe that he was entitled to claim New Zealand for King George III. The official claim was enacted on a small hill above the watering place, overlooking a grove of pohutukawa trees and Cook's Bay.

Today the eastern bank of the Purangi River estuary can be accessed at the very end of Lees Road, which branches from the road linking Purangi Road with the road to Hahei. Lees Road climbs through farmland and orchards before descending to a track which leads down to the Stella Evered Memorial Park and a landing on the eastern bank of the Purangi River. The park is administered as a publicly accessible natural, cultural and historic reserve. From its western shore at low tide the Purangi River can be waded or crossed easily in a dinghy, to access the eastern shore.

What did the Maori people think of the strange arrivals and their huge canoe? Unsurprisingly, they considered the visitors with their pale skins, strange clothing and exploding walking sticks, supernatural beings. The name they used for the outlandish creatures was 'tupua', meaning in English, 'goblins'.[3]

There was a brisk trade between the men of *Endeavour* and the Ngati Hei, the latter being keen to obtain Tahitian bark cloth, and Cook and his men bartering for quantities of fish and shellfish. The oysters in particular the Englishmen found superb. Also, many shags were shot, and found to be delicious eating.

Although relations between the men of *Endeavour* and Mercury Bay Maori were mainly amicable, one local man was shot and killed by Lieutenant John Gore, after he bartered for the man's dogskin cloak with a length of cloth. Gore handed the cloth over but the Maori man retained his cloak. Furious, Gore aimed his musket, fired, and killed him. Considering this action out of all proportion to the act the victim had committed, Cook and Banks both admonished Gore for the killing. In his usual understated manner Cook wrote that the act 'did not meet with my approbation.'[4] Fortunately the shooting did not impair relations with the Ngati Hei, who remained on friendly terms with the visitors throughout their stay. It is said that the man Gore killed was buried in his dogskin cloak.

Horeta Te Taniwha was a small boy visiting Mercury Bay in November 1769. Eighty-three years later, in 1852, he recounted to the New Zealand Lieutenant-Governor, Robert Henry Wynyard:

> *There was one supreme man in that ship. We knew that he was the lord of the whole by his perfect gentlemanly and noble demeanour. But this man did not utter many words: all that he did was to handle our mats and hold our mere, spears and wahaika [hand weapon] and touch the hair of our heads. He was a very good man, and came to us—the children—and patted our cheeks, and gently touched our heads.[5]*

Mercury Bay was charted thoroughly during *Endeavour*'s visit, and excursions made into the surrounding area, including a probing of Whitianga harbour, which Cook named 'Mangrove River'.

SHAKESPEARE CLIFF

At the western end of Cook's Beach the land rises steeply to a high headland, called Shakespeare Cliff Scenic and Historic Reserve. A drive leads off the Purangi Road to the reserve. At the entrance to the drive are memorial gates, erected in 1969 to commemorate the bicentenary of Cook's visit to the district and his observation of the transit of Mercury. In 1970 a royal picnic was held in a paddock near the Shakespeare Cliff car park. Queen Elizabeth II and her royal entourage visited the area to help celebrate the Cook bicentenary.

The road climbs through bush to a car park, from where it is a short walk up to the lookout.

The Shakespeare Cliff reserve has groves of ancient pohutukawa trees, picnic areas, striking rock formations and a network of paths leading down to white sand beaches inaccessible by road. A lookout at the top of the cliff provides vistas of Mercury Bay and Cook's Beach. Information boards around the lookout platform describe the historical provenance of the area and the location of the various natural features that can be viewed from it. Lonely Bay, accessible only on foot or by water, is a beautiful cove between the lookout and the western end of Cook's Beach.

Parking for visitors to Shakespeare Cliff is available at various locations, including picturesque Flaxmill Bay, at the base of the western end of the cliff. A track at the eastern end of the bay leads up to and along the headland to a grassy reserve with pohutukawa trees, before connecting at the opposite end with an unsealed road to the lookout at the top of the headland. Hikers should allow at least an hour to walk this three-kilometre return loop.

At the very end of Purangi Road is Whitianga Rock, a pa site on the Ferry Landing side of the Whitianga River. The site is a peninsula protected on three of its sides by sheer cliffs. The fourth side of the peninsula is defended by a seven-metre, man-made trench, which now comprises part of the track leading to Back Bay, where the pa's inhabitants could collect shellfish. According to Ngati Hei history, the earliest known occupier of the pa site was Hei Turepe.

James Cook visited the Whitianga pa site during his stay in Mercury Bay. Of it he commented, 'The situation is such that the best Engineers in Europe could not have choose'd a better site for a small number of men to defend themselves against a greater...'[6]

Cook noted the burnt stumps of a palisade, evidence that a battle had evicted the pa's original inhabitants. The local people confirmed to Cook that the pa had been disused for some years, after it was attacked by a chief from Tauranga. He killed the local leader, spared his wife, married her, then settled in with the Ngati Hei tribe at another location.

A track leading to the top of Whitianga Rock begins on the fourth side of the peninsula, near the Ferry Landing carpark. From the top of the rock there are wide views of the Whitianga River, the harbour and Whitianga town.

On 12 November 1769 Cook and a party from *Endeavour* also visited two pa sites at the western end of Mercury Bay. These were called Te Puta O Paretauhinau and Wharetaewa and they lie at either end of Wharekaho Beach, which is commonly known today as Simpson's Beach. Cook named it 'Cellery Cove'.

Wharetaewa Pa occupied the headland at the southern end of Wharekaho Beach. When Cook's party visited it was heavily palisaded and occupied by about a hundred people. They were friendly towards the visitors and gifts were exchanged.

Even more spectacular Te Puta O Paretauhinau ('The Hole of Paretauhinau'), was at the northern end of the beach, atop an arched rock that was cut off from the mainland at high tide. There were only a few houses on top of the arch, but the site was so striking that Banks described it as 'the most beautifully romantick thing

I ever saw.'[7] The visitors from *Endeavour* named the pa 'Sporing's Grotto' after Herman Sporing, one of *Endeavour*'s naturalists. The arch of Te Puta O Paretauhinau has long since crumbled and fallen into the sea, and the rest of the site has been largely eroded away, but its strategic advantages can still be appreciated today.

Wharekaho-Simpson's Beach is today accessed via SH 25, on the way north after the highway passes through Whitianga town. It then crosses the Ake Ake River, which flows into the sea near the southern end of the beach. Wharekaho Beach was renamed 'Simpson's Beach' after a pioneer family who lived in the district.

The site of what was Wharetaewa Pa can be seen on the headland at the southern end of Wharekaho-Simpson's Beach. The remains of the pa site terracing, a distinctive layering of the headland's hillside, is noticeable. Today the headland is known as 'Davis Point', so named after a local Maori family. A well-known Wharekaho-Simpson's Beach resident is Joe Davis, a Ngati Hei kaumatua—a respected tribal elder.

There are no shops at Wharekaho-Simpson's Beach, but holiday accommodation is available for rental.

THE CATHEDRAL COVE WALK

The Cathedral Cove Walk, which begins above the beachside settlement of Hahei, is one of the most popular walks in the Coromandel. Indeed, it has become so popular that it pays to start the walk very early, in order to avoid the vehicles that crowd the car park and the people who mass along the track and at the cove.

From the shopping centre in Hahei, follow Grange Road, which leads up the hill to the lookout car park. There is also access to the car park from a coastal track at the northern end of Hahei beach.

Allow an extra 20–30 minutes if taking this steep track. Below the car park there is an excellent lookout platform and a series of information boards.

From the car park the track descends gradually into a valley where a side loop takes walkers through a grove of ancient puriri trees (*Vitex lucens*), then back onto the main track.

Other tracks branch off the main trail. They lead to Gemstone Bay, Stingray Bay and Mare's Leg Cove, which are all worth a detour. However the north-western end of the beach at Stingray Bay is closed due to the danger of falling rocks and debris from the cliffs above. It is not advisable to go to this end of the beach or its nearby waters. At Gemstone Bay there is a boulder beach and a snorkel trail. The bay was named for the brightly coloured stones that can be found among the boulders. A little further on, at the end of another side track, is Stingray Bay. Here there are some boulders but also a sandy beach, a sea cave and intricate weathering of the cliff face above the bay.

Returning to the main track, the path climbs out of the valley and up to an elevated area that overlooks the coastline and offshore islands. The track then crosses scrubland and passes through a pine forest. Then it descends via a series of steps down to Cathedral Cove itself.

Cathedral Cove's name derives from the fact that it has a natural rock arch connecting it to Mare's Leg Cove. Over time, sea erosion will cause the arch to collapse, so that it will form an offshore 'stack'. Take care when walking through the arch separating the two beaches at Cathedral Cove, as rockfall hazards exist in the vicinity of the arch because of weathering and eroding of the rock. There is a solitary stack at the western end of Cathedral Cove, called 'Te Horo Rock'.

The coastline from Hahei to Cathedral Cove comprises part of the Te Whanganui-A-Hei Marine Reserve, which was established in 1992. Within the reserve all marine life is protected, to encourage the sea life within it to breed and thus maintain the rich and diverse aquatic habitats of the area. Signs around the coast draw attention to the reserve and emphasise the importance of maintaining the ban on the taking of fish and shellfish from it.

Track overview: 2.5 kilometres, 1 hour 30 minutes return. No dogs.

Website: www.doc.govt.nz/parks-and-recreation/places-to-go/coromandel/places/hahei-area/tracks/cathedral-cove-walk.

A proposed longer Cathedral Coast walk

A coastal walk from Cathedral Cove west to the Purangi River mouth is in the planning stages. A boardwalk will cross the rocky coastline from Cathedral Cove to below Cook Bluff, then on to the estuary of the Purangi River and to Cook Bay. Construction of the proposed boardwalk over the rocky sections of the coast will require consents from the Waikato Regional Council.

Ultimately it is intended that this walk will be part of a Great Coromandel Walk that will connect Whitianga, Cooks Beach, Cathedral Cove and Hahei with Hot Water Beach.

For the latest information about the progress of the proposed walk, check the website: www.tcdc.govt.nz/ccwalk.

WHITIANGA

Whitianga (population 4100) is the main urban centre of Mercury Bay and the eastern Coromandel. The original name of the town site was Te Whitianga O Kupe, meaning 'Kupe's Crossing Place', a tribute to Kupe, the great Polynesian voyager.

During the second half of the nineteenth century Whitianga was a busy mill town and kauri timber export port. Today it is a service centre and tourist hub, with a large marina, a variety of holiday accommodation, an extensive retail sector, a regional museum and fishing boat charter facilities.

The town is reached either from a turn-off right at crossroads at Whenuakite on SH 25, or from an inland route via Coroglen, also on SH 25. The Whenuakite turn-off leads to Hot Water Beach Road, then Purangi Road branches off to the left. Purangi Road leads to Whitianga, first passing Cooks Beach, then terminating just above Whitianga harbour and river mouth. The stone Ferry Landing on the eastern side of the harbour is one of the oldest constructions in New Zealand, dating from 1837. A public ferry service across the harbour began in 1895. Today Whitianga town can be reached from the Ferry Landing via a modern, 63-seat passenger ferry, *Diana Rose,* which makes the short return crossing of the river every fifteen minutes.

The Whitianga ferry runs from 7.30am to 7.30pm, then from 8.30pm to 10.30pm, daily.

Following the quick ferry trip across the river, from the wharf it is a short walk to Whitianga's town centre. On its eastern side the town is fronted by five-kilometre-long Buffalo Beach, named after HMS *Buffalo,* which was wrecked in a storm while anchored in Mercury Bay in July 1840.

70

Well worth a visit is the Mercury Bay Museum, opposite the jetty on the town side of the river. The museum's walls are painted with murals depicting the kauri milling era and the two great navigators, the Polynesian Kupe and the Englishman James Cook. Inside the museum are several Cook-related exhibits. A range of books on Coromandel history are for sale at the museum, along with a CD entitled *Twelve Days—Captain James Cook in Mercury Bay*. This features the events that occurred during *Endeavour*'s sojourn in the bay in November 1769.

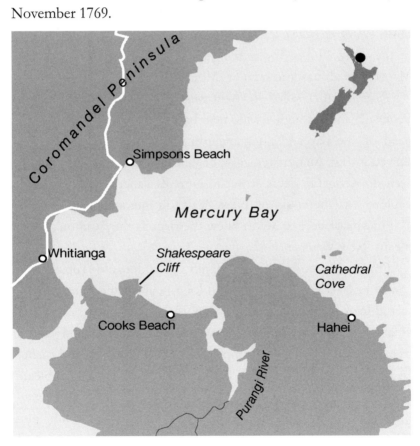

Map of Mercury Bay

ENDEAVOUR'S VOYAGE:
INTO THE FIRTH OF THAMES

Endeavour's stay in Mercury Bay had been mostly helpful and hospitable. The ship had been provedored; it was now time to sail on. At 7am on 16 November 1769, *Endeavour*'s anchors were weighed and Cook took her northwards. Four days later she doubled the northern tip of the Coromandel Peninsula. Cook named this landform 'Cape Colvill' after Alexander Colvill, 7th Baron Colvill (1717–1770). He had been Cook's commander on HMS *Northumberland,* a ship on which he served as sailing master in the early 1760s. Today the cape's name is spelled 'Colville'. Maori have always known it as 'Moehau'.

Endeavour then sailed down the western coast of the Coromandel Peninsula and through a wide tidal bay. Cook took the ship to the head of the bay and after anchoring saw that a navigable river flowed into it. Mangroves grew prolifically on its margins. Having seen no navigable rivers so far in New Zealand, Cook decided to explore what he could of New Zealand's interior, using the river as a means of access. Maori knew the river as the 'Waihou', which means 'New Waters'.

On 20 November Cook, Banks, Solander and Tupaia were rowed in *Endeavour*'s pinnace and long boat up the river, moving inland for several miles on a flowing tide. Cook's party saw to their amazement that the mangroves were giving way to stands of tall trees, soaring out of the swampy growth of raupo, flax and rushes. In Banks's description, 'The banks of the river were compleatly cloathed with the finest timber my Eyes ever beheld'.[8] These were mainly the New Zealand native tree, kahikatea, or white pine (*Dacrycarpus dacrydioides*).

After the party landed on the west bank of the river, about twenty kilometres from the sea, Cook measured one of the trees. Its girth was around six metres, from its base to the first branch it measured 27 metres and its trunk was as 'streight as an arrow', Cook wrote. A perfect timber for ships' masts, he decided. There was another tree species growing here. It was heavy and solid. This was the matai, or black pine (*Prumnopitys taxifolia*), which although too heavy for masts would be suitable for ship's planking.

After naming the river and the bay after London's Thames, Cook and his party returned to *Endeavour* on an ebbing tide. The ship and crew then left the Coromandel and resumed their northward course.

Although Cook's exploration of the interior of New Zealand had been brief, his and Banks's description of the fine timber stands of the area drained by the Thames River—whose name reverted to 'Waihou' in 1928—was to have far-reaching consequences for the entire Coromandel region.

The Waihou River today meanders across the low-lying Hauraki Plains before it debouches into the Firth of Thames. Over the last 150 years the swampy plain has been laboriously drained and is now given over to farmland, mainly for dairying and fodder crops. There are only patches of trees remaining, almost all exotic species.

So where did the great native forests go?

Alerted to the presence of the fine timber trees by Cook and Banks's published journals, entrepreneurs were not slow to cross the world and exploit this valuable resource. In 1794 English sea captain Thomas Dell arrived in the Firth of Thames in the ship *Fancy*. He and his crew sailed up the Thames River and disembarked at a heavily forested area where a tributary met it. They called the place 'Graves End'; Maori called it 'Hikutaia'. Dell and his men were there for three months. With assistance from local Maori, and in exchange for some iron goods, Dell's men felled 213 kahikatea trees. The logs were shipped away for spars, along with quantities of flax for cordage. The plundering of the region's natural resources was under way.

Once clothed in forest, mainly kauri, matai and kahikatea, most of the Coromandel peninsula's magnificent trees were felled and milled during the late nineteenth and early twentieth century. The timber, especially that derived from the superb giant kauri (*Agathis australis*), was used for the building of houses, ships and furniture in the growing towns of young New Zealand, mainly Auckland. Later the discovery of quartz gold in 1867 around Thames led to more wholesale environmental damage on the Coromandel Peninsula. The only native trees left were those in the inaccessible areas of its ruggedly mountainous interior. Those remaining trees are now protected.

Today the tiny, eastern Hauraki Plains settlement of Hikutaia is on SH 26. The Waihou River flows into the Firth of Thames near the small town of Kopu, four kilometres south of Thames (7140), which is the main urban centre of the western Coromandel.

SH 26 connects Thames and Paeroa, a town ten kilometres south of Hikutaia, at the junction of SH 26 and SH 2.

Paeroa's Historic Maritime Park

North-west of Paeroa, on SH 2, is an Historical Maritime Park. As New Zealand's only inland port, Paeroa has important links to New Zealand's past, including pre-European settlement, James Cook's voyage up the Waihou River and the gold and timber rushes in the region during the nineteenth century. Housed in a heritage building beside a tributary of the Waihou River, the park holds many exhibits pertaining to local maritime history. Opening hours Monday to Sunday, 10am to 3pm. Email: hmp@outlook.co.nz. Website: www.historicalmaritimepark.co.nz.

COOK'S LANDING, NETHERTON

On SH 2, travelling south from Auckland towards Paeroa, is the settlement of Netherton. This marked the furthest inland point of Cook's upriver expedition on 20 November 1769. The event is marked by a stone cairn and Cook's Landing Reserve, near a bank of the Waihou River. The reserve is on the corner of SH 2 and Captain Cook Road, just before Netherton itself. The monument is crowned with an anchor donated by the New Zealand Navy.

THE MERCURY ISLANDS

This group of seven islands is eight kilometres off the eastern coast of the Coromandel Peninsula, and 35 kilometres north-east of Whitianga town. Named after the transit of Mercury observed by James Cook and his astronomer Charles Green on 9 November 1769, the seven islands are: Great Mercury-Ahuahu, Red Mercury-Whakau, and much smaller Korapuki, Green, Middle-Atiu, Stanley-Kawhutu and Double-Moturehu. The islands are the remnants of an ancient volcano.

Only Great Mercury is inhabited, the others are part of a nature reserve. Great Mercury is privately owned by two prominent New Zealand businessmen, but is open to the public. In 2014 a programme was begun, funded by Great Mercury's owners and the Department of Conservation, to make the island predator-free. Two years later it was announced that the Great

Mercury group was free of introduced mammalian pests such as rats and mustelids.

The smaller islands in the Mercury group provide safe nesting sites for thousands of breeding pairs of Pycroft's petrels (*Pterodroma pycrofti*), while Double Island-Moturehu and Red Mercury-Whakau are home to the critically endangered insect species, the Mercury Islands tusked weta (*Motuweta isolate*).

Piercy Island and the 'Hole in the Rock', off Cape Brett, Bay of Islands

CHAPTER FOUR

THE NORTH-EAST COAST

In this Skirmish only one or two of them was Hurt with small Shot.

ENDEAVOUR'S VOYAGE: THE NORTH-EAST COAST

A serious omission from James Cook's traverse of the Hauraki Gulf in November 1769 was that he never entered one of its major branches, the Waitemata Harbour. Today Auckland, New Zealand's largest city and principal port, is located on the Tamaki isthmus and around the shores of the Waitemata Harbour.

Cook only missed the Waitemata Harbour by a few nautical miles. On 23 November he anchored *Endeavour* off the north-east point of Waiheke Island, one of the largest in the Hauraki Gulf. He charted sections of the Waiheke coastline and neighbouring Ponui Island, but did not venture further west. However Cook shrewdly surmised of the islands that, 'it appear'd very probable that these form'd some good harbours likewise.'[1]

Had he sailed 21.5 kilometres further west from

Waiheke Island Cook would surely have noted the suitability of the deep, sheltered Waitemata Harbour as a port. Later, in 1840, the English governor Captain William Hobson did discern the harbour's advantages and for this reason chose Auckland as the site of New Zealand's capital.

On the western side of the Tamaki isthmus was another large harbour, the Manukau. Exposed to the prevailing south-west winds, this harbour's entrance is often hazardous. In mid-January 1770 Cook would have sailed past the Manukau's bar, but keeping *Endeavour* well out from the west coast's lee shore, he almost certainly missed seeing this harbour's entrance.

Maori knew the Tamaki isthmus as 'Tamaki-makau-rau', which translates as 'Tamaki having one hundred lovers', testimony to the area's desirability for its original inhabitants. In two places the isthmus was so narrow—just a few kilometres across—that Maori could portage their canoes from one harbour to the other, in effect travelling from the east coast of Te-Ika-A-Maui to its west coast, or vice versa.

Auckland retained its capital status until 1865, when this role was passed to more central Wellington. But Auckland remains New Zealand's largest city by far, with a population of 1.5 million, and is the country's main commercial and industrial centre.

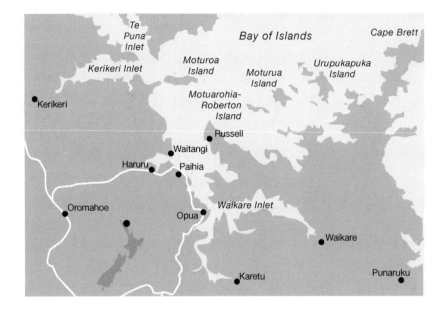

Map of Cape Brett to Kerikeri

WAIHEKE ISLAND

Waiheke is the second largest island in the Hauraki Gulf, after Great Barrier Island. Waiheke is the more populous, however, with 8730 permanent residents. During the holiday season from December to February the population swells to over 12,000, with many Aucklanders staying in holiday homes on the island.

Waiheke has become home to many wealthy people in recent years, and their palatial homes can be seen atop the hills and around the coasts. Most of the island's population is concentrated at its western end, where the main town, Oneroa, is located. Here there is a variety of shops, several cafes and restaurants and an excellent library. From the main street of Oneroa there are beautiful views

81

looking north across the Hauraki Gulf to Little Barrier and Great Barrier Islands.

Waiheke is noted for its many fine beaches and secluded bays, particularly on its northern coasts. Oneroa and Onetangi are the best-known of these, but between them are several others, such as Little Oneroa, Sandy Bay, Enclosure Bay and Mawhitipana Bay, which is fronted by Palm Beach. Waiheke is very popular with boaties, and in summer the bays become crowded with yachts and launches, in particular the bay below Oneroa town.

The climate of Waiheke—drier and sunnier than the mainland—is ideal for grape growing. There are many vineyards on the island, producing the fine wines Waiheke is noted for, and several of the wineries incorporate quality restaurants. The wines produced on the island are predominantly red (57%), the main varietals being merlot (19%) and syrah (18%). The main white varietals are chardonnay (16%), sauvignon blanc (12%) and pinot gris (10%). The best known of the vineyards are Mudbrick, Stonyridge, Te Whau and Cable Bay. Wine tours of Waiheke are a great way to see the island.

Regular passenger and vehicle ferry services connect Auckland with Waiheke. The passenger ferries leave from the Downtown terminal in Auckland's Quay Street and take 40 minutes to reach the island's terminal at Matiatia, at the western end of Waiheke. Vehicle ferries leave from the Wynyard Quarter near Downtown Auckland and from Half Moon Bay, on the Tamaki estuary in east Auckland, and berth at Kennedy Point, on the island's south-west coast.

For more information about visiting Waiheke Island, refer to the website: www.waiheke.co.nz.

TWO BARRIER ISLANDS

After *Endeavour* brushed past Waiheke Island's east coast, a south-westerly gale carried Cook's ship north. She then came upon two islands, one much larger than the other. Cook named them 'Great Barrier' and 'Little Barrier'. Maori knew Great Barrier as Aotea and Little Barrier as Hauturu. Although Cook did not land on either island, he appreciated the 'barrier' their craggy profiles afforded *Endeavour* from the strong winds.

Located on the northern edge of the Hauraki Gulf, Great Barrier is New Zealand's sixth largest island. It has an area of 285 square kilometre and its outlying islands include Kaikoura-Selwyn, Rakitu-Arid and Aiguilles-Needles Point. The interior of 'the Barrier' is very rugged and rises to its highest point at Mount Hobson, 621 metres above sea level.

In the nineteenth century Great Barrier Island was exploited for its stands of fine kauri trees. They were felled in the interior, then dams were built across the island's streams and their waters were impounded. The dams were then 'tripped' (broken) and the logs were swept down by the water and along the stream beds to the coast. There they were rafted and towed to Auckland for milling, to provide timber for housing and ships. However the kauri dam system of log transportation caused great damage to the island's environment.

The east coast of Great Barrier Island, which is exposed to the Pacific Ocean, has long, white sand beaches, sand dunes and heavy surf. The west coast, being more sheltered, has many small bays suitable for boating, fishing and diving. Port Fitzroy, a long sheltered sound at the north-western end of the island, leads to a harbourside settlement of the same name. Another entry channel,

Man of War passage, provides access to Port Fitzroy from the Hauraki Gulf.

Today the population of Great Barrier is about 1000 and the island's main economic activities are farming and tourism. Visitors to the island often feel they have stepped back in time by about half a century, because of the laid-back way of life and the absence of modern facilities. About 60 per cent of the island is administered as a nature reserve by the Department of Conservation and its native forests are regenerating. The island's harbours, particularly Port Fitzroy in the north and Tryphena in the south, are very popular bases for cruising yachts and launches. Hiking tracks lace the island's interior and the climb to Mt Hobson, although gruelling, provides panoramic views of the island and its coastline.

Passenger and vehicle ferries connect central Auckland with Tryphena. There are scheduled air services to the island's airports at Claris and Okiwi from Auckland Airport and the North Shore Aerodrome, beside SH 1 at Dairy Flat.

Transport and accommodation options can be viewed at the website: www.greatbarrierislandtourism.co.nz.

Little Barrier Island is an andesitic volcano, roughly circular in shape. It rises very steeply to 722 metres above sea level and is densely forested. The island's total land area is 28 square kilometres and the only flat land is at Te Toki Point, on its west coast.

Little Barrier was declared a wildlife sanctuary in 1897, New Zealand's first. Today, access to the island is restricted. Only Department of Conservation staff, rangers and scientists can live on Little Barrier and permits must be obtained from the Department of Conservation for those who wish to visit the island. Free of predatory rats and feral cats since 2004, the ecosystem of Little

Barrier is now very close to that of New Zealand before the arrival of any human beings, Maori or Pakeha. Within the island's forested habitat a range of indigenous plant, bird and insect species thrives, including the critically endangered kakapo. Little Barrier is also home to New Zealand's unique endemic reptile, the tuatara.

Long, undulating Great Barrier Island, and steep-sided, conic Little Barrier Island are both visible from the Auckland isthmus on a clear day.

Website: www.doc.govt.nz/littlebarrierisland.

CAPE RODNEY-OKAKARI POINT MARINE RESERVE

Continuing her voyage along the east coast of the North Island, *Endeavour* passed a promontory named by Cook 'Cape Rodney', after George Brydges Rodney, an English naval hero.

Today this place is the Cape Rodney-Okakari Point Marine Reserve. Opened in 1977, it was New Zealand's first such reserve, occupying 518 hectares of the coast. The University of Auckland has a research facility here, called the Leigh Marine Laboratory.

The reserve is very popular with snorkelers, as fish such as blue maomao, snapper and parore thrive in its protected waters and can be seen close-up. It is also possible to take a tour of the reserve in a glass-bottom boat. The grassy area above the marine reserve makes a pleasant picnic spot. Consequently both the sea and the shore become very crowded at weekends.

The Cape Rodney-Okakari Point Marine Reserve is reached by turning right at Warkworth, on SH 1, then passing through the small settlements of Matakana and Leigh. From Leigh it is only a short drive north to Goat Island Bay.

Website: www.discovergoatisland.co.nz/reserve.html.

BREAM BAY

Bream Bay is a wide cove on the east coast of Northland, enclosed by Bream Tail to the south and Bream Head to the north. Both landmarks were named by Cook. There are two townships on the bay's coast, Waipu and Ruakaka. Marsden Point, an important industrial port, lies opposite Bream Head at the entrance to Whangarei Harbour.

On 24 November 1769, *Endeavour*'s anchor was lowered in Bream Bay. The crew dropped lines overboard and nearly 100 fish were caught. Cook used the generic term 'bream' to describe these fish, but they were probably snapper or tarakihi, among New Zealand's best eating fish. Cook named the bay in recognition of his crew's big catch. Cook also made note of the striking 'peeked rocks rainged in order' on the top of Bream Head, but in the early morning light he did not see the entrance to Whangarei Harbour.

Waipu Cove, just north of Bream Tail, is a fine swimming beach, best reached by a secondary road via Mangawhai Heads, a popular coastal holiday settlement. From Mangawhai Heads the road cuts inland, heads north, then joins the coast at another attractive destination, Lang's Beach, south of Waipu Cove.

THE HEN AND CHICKENS ISLANDS

This group of islands lies twelve kilometres east of Bream Head. They were named the Hen and Chickens by Cook, it is thought because they resembled the old name for the star cluster, Pleiades. Maori knew this star group as Matariki. However the islands do resemble a mother hen protecting a row of her chickens.

The Hen and Chickens Islands were owned originally by the northern Maori tribe, Nga Puhi, who sold them to the New

Zealand government in 1883. In 1908 the islands were declared a scenic reserve in view of their rare flora and fauna, and in 1953 they became a wildlife sanctuary.

There are seven islands in the group: Hen-Taranga, Muriwhenua, Wareware, Lady Alice, Whatupuke, Coppermine and Mauataha.

Long, narrow and craggy, Hen-Taranga is by far the largest of the seven. Her dominant feature is a rocky ridge that rises to 417 metres above sea level. This formation is known as 'The Pinnacles'. Sail Rock, a stack three kilometres south of Hen-Taranga, is a prominent navigational focus for sailors.

The Hen and Chickens are noted for their avian life. These include seabirds and forest birds which have become rare or extinct on the mainland. Hen-Taranga Island is one of the few places in New Zealand which has a surviving population of North Island saddlebacks. Because they are home to a breeding population of about 500 pairs of Pycroft's petrels, the Hen and Chickens have been declared an Important Bird Area by Birdlife International.

On a fine day there are views of the Hen and Chickens from the Mangawhai Cliffs walk, and from the Brynderwyn Hills, on SH 1 north of Kaiwaka.

THE POOR KNIGHTS ISLANDS

This island chain lies off the coast of Northland, twenty kilometres directly east of the small settlement of Whananaki and 23 kilometres north-east of the resort township of Tutukaka. The islands are the eroded remnants of an ancient rhyolitic volcano.

The group consists of two large islands, Tawhiti Rahi, which is slightly larger than Aorangi, and a cluster of islets between the two.

The largest of these is Motu Kapiti. The Poor Knights were so-named by Cook when he sailed past the group on 25 November 1769. The name was chosen possibly because Tawhiti Rahi resembles the shape of a prone person. An alternative explanation is the islands' resemblance in shape to Poor Knight's Pudding, a bread-based dessert dish popular in late-eighteenth century England.

The Poor Knights group was once occupied by a hapu (sub-tribe) of the Ngati Wai people, but became uninhabited after the 1820s. Feral pigs once roamed on Aorangi, but these were exterminated by 1936.

Today the islands are a nature sanctuary surrounded by the Poor Knights' Islands Marine Reserve. A permit is required to tie boats up or for people to land, and this is only granted for the purposes of scientific research.

The water around the Poor Knights is very deep, with only moderate tidal currents, and is famed for its clarity and abundance of marine life. This makes diving and snorkelling in the marine reserve an exceptional experience. The renowned marine biologist the late Jacques Cousteau rated the waters around the Poor Knights among the top-ten dive sites in the world.

Fish commonly seen in the waters surrounding the islands include banded wrasse, blue moki, butterfish, butterfly perch, moray eels, parore, kingfish, silver drummer and porcupine fish.

On land, a unique plant species that grows on the islands is the beautiful Flowering Poor Knights lily.

Purpose-built dive boats depart from the Tutukaka Marina daily at 8am for the Poor Knights, returning at about 4.30pm. Cruise boats also depart from Tutukaka and from the water passengers can take in the islands' scenery, marine life and sea birds.

Phone: Freephone 0800 288 882. Websites: diving.co.nz/poor-knights-islands; www.aperfectday.co.nz.

CAPE BRETT

Cape Brett caps the end of a long, narrow peninsula extending into the Pacific Ocean. The peninsula marks the southern entrance to the Bay of Islands.

Two kilometres east of Cape Brett is Piercy Island, which is penetrated by a large hole. After Cook's *Endeavour* reached the cape on 28 November 1769, Cook named it in honour of Rear Admiral Sir Piercy Brett, one of the three Lords of the Admiralty who had signed his secret instructions before he left on the voyage. In a rare venture into punning, Cook named the island 'Piercy', after its hole, which in his words, 'perced (sic) quite thro' it like the Arch of a Bridge.'[3]

After rounding Cape Brett, Cook took *Endeavour* past a large bay containing many islands. The ship continued sailing north past the bay, then came to a group of rocky islands just off the coast. Maori came out in canoes and traded cavalle (horse mackerel) with the ship's company. This led Cook to name the group the 'Cavalles'. Today they are known as the Cavalli Islands.

Later the same day the wind turned to the north, driving *Endeavour* back southward. And on the morning of 29 November 1769 Cook's ship entered the broad, sheltered cove that he had already named, 'The Bay of Islands'.

The Cape Brett Track

The Cape Brett Track crosses rugged terrain and passes through regenerating native forest. It first runs along a ridge through Maori-owned land before coming to Conservation

Department land. A side track can be taken to Deep Water Cove (one hour return), which is a good swimming and snorkelling spot. From Deep Water Cove onwards the track becomes more challenging, being exposed and with steep drop-offs to the sea. However, from the peninsula's forested ridges there are dramatic views of coastal scenery. An electric fence crosses the peninsula, to reduce the impact of possums on the native forest. Trampers must always ensure that the gate through the fence is kept closed.

The going on the latter stages of the track is tougher, but the views—north to the Cavalli Islands, east to the Poor Knights and south to Whangaruru—compensate for the effort.

There is a lighthouse on the cape. It is now automated, and the keeper's house is a tramper's hut. It is serviced, has 23 bunk beds, mattresses and cooking facilities but no eating utensils. Bookings are required.

The track is twenty kilometres long; track time is six-eight hours each way.

Website: www.capebrettwalks.co.nz.

THE BAY OF ISLANDS

The Bay of Islands is one of the New Zealand's best-known holiday destinations. A fine natural harbour, it is famed for its harbour cruises, swimming with dolphins, sea kayaking and big-game fishing. The area surrounding the bay also has many places of historic interest.

The bay itself is sixteen kilometres wide. Within it are 144 islands, the largest of which is Urupukapuka. Several peninsulas extend into the bay and around its shores are many coves and inlets.

Urban developments are all on the mainland, leaving the islands largely in their natural state.

The bay and the land surrounding it were occupied by Maori since about the fourteenth century. They knew the area as 'Ipipiri'. Among the many resources which attracted Maori settlement were a subtropical climate and a hinterland with fertile volcanic soils for the growing of crops such as kumara, taro, yams and fernroot. Forests of miro, totara, rimu and kahikatea hosted birdlife and provided timber for the building of houses and large waka (canoes).

The estuaries of the rivers that drained into the bay provided sheltered canoe anchorages and its headlands were ideal for the building of fortified villages. The waters of the bay teemed with fish. It was little wonder that the Bay of Islands was New Zealand's most densely populated area when the first Europeans arrived.

Cook and *Endeavour*'s company were not slow to appreciate the natural benefits of the Bay of Islands. After climbing a hill on Motuarohia, the first island he and Cook landed on, naturalist Joseph Banks noted:

> *The bay we were in was indeed a most surprising place: it was full of an innumerable quantity of Islands forming as many harbours, which must be as smooth as mill pools as they Landlock one another numberless times. Every where round us we could see large Indian towns, houses and cultivations: we had certainly seen no place near so populous as this one was very near us.[3]*

The Bay of Islands also became the site of the first permanent European settlement in New Zealand. After Cook's charting and documentation of the bay were published in Europe, whalers, traders and adventurers of many kinds washed up on its shores. A town sprang up on the largest peninsula and functioned mainly as a provisioning port for whaling ships. Called 'Kororareka', it was the first permanent town established in New Zealand. During the first decades of the nineteenth century Kororareka became notorious for its dissoluteness, lawlessness and violence. Today the town is called Russell, and it is one of the New Zealand's most desirable holiday destinations.

Along with the whalers and traders, Protestant and Catholic missionaries arrived in the Bay of Islands, eager to convert the Maori to Christianity. The first to come was the English protestant Samuel Marsden, who arrived in 1814. Subsequently other missionaries set up stations around the bay and succeeded in converting many Maori. The Bible was translated into the Maori language and a press at Kororareka printed the scriptures and other documents. The town of Kerikeri, just north of the Bay of Islands, was the site of the first permanent mission station in New Zealand.

Today Kerikeri has several buildings dating from the earliest European settlement in New Zealand. The town's Mission House, also known as the Kemp House (built in 1821), is the oldest surviving wooden structure in New Zealand, and the nearby Stone Store (built in 1836) is the oldest stone building in the country. Rewi's Village, just across the river from the Stone Store, is a reconstruction of a traditional kainga, an unfortified Maori village like the ones Cook and his men observed and described in 1769. Rewi's Village is a centre for the display of traditional Maori culture.

At Waimate North, between Kerikeri and Lake Omapere, inland west of the Bay of Islands, is Te Waimate North Mission House. This restored colonial residence also dates from the early nineteenth century, although the nearby St John the Baptist Church was built much later.

In spite of the arrival of the missionaries and European settlers, lawlessness around the Bay of Islands continued. Relations between the Europeans and Maori deteriorated, mainly as a result of unscrupulous land dealings. Also, the French, Britain's traditional foe, were threatening to colonise New Zealand. Mainly to bring law and order to the region, and to forestall French imperial expansion, in 1833 the London authorities dispatched a British Resident, James Busby, to the Bay of Islands. However mainly because he was inadequately resourced, Busby's authority proved ineffectual.

Seven years later Captain William Hobson was sent to the Bay of Islands to replace Busby, and to persuade the Maori chiefs to cede sovereignty to the British Crown, in exchange for its protection of them. Hobson arrived in the bay from Sydney, on 29 January 1840. A treaty was subsequently drawn up, detailing the rights and obligations of both parties. After lengthy debate and some amendment, the treaty was signed, on 6 February 1840, accompanied by considerable ceremony. The place of signing was Waitangi, on the western shore of the Bay of Islands.

Today this place is considered one of the most important historic sites in New Zealand and 6 February, Waitangi Day, is a national holiday. On this day the two marae at Waitangi become the focus of both official celebrations of the signing of the Treaty and protests by those Maori who consider its obligations have not been honoured by the Crown.

A new Museum of Waitangi was opened in 2016. Full of interesting displays, many of them interactive, the exhibits tell the story of early Maori and European contacts as well as the ongoing development of New Zealand as a sovereign nation.

Today the Bay of Islands is the North Island's aquatic playground. Water-based activities of every kind are available, from big game fishing to swimming with dolphins. All these activities make the most of the bay's many natural assets.

The best way to explore the bay is to see it from the water. A cruise allows the visitor to see the places which Cook first charted: Cape Brett, Piercy Island-the Hole in the Rock, Motuarohia-Roberton Island, Moturua Island, the Orokawa Peninsula and other landmarks in between. When weather conditions permit, cruise boats pass through the 'Hole in the Rock'.

A sheltered bay on Motuarohia-Roberton Island, where Cook's party came ashore, is today a favourite anchorage for pleasure craft. A bay on the island's southern shore is called 'Cooks Cove'. Pine trees now grow on the headland at the eastern tip of the island where there was a palisaded pa, sketched by Herman Sporing in 1769.

Waipao Bay on neighbouring Moturua Island, where Cook's men filled *Endeavour*'s water casks, is a fine swimming beach.

Three years after Cook and *Endeavour* visited the Bay of Islands, terrible events occurred in the same area.

On a peninsula opposite Moturua Island is a bay called Assassination Cove, also known as Te Hue Bay. This was the place where French navigator Marc-Joseph Marion du Fresne (1724–1772) and 26 of his men were killed and eaten, on 12 June 1772.

The Frenchmen were visiting the Bay of Islands in two ships, the *Mascarin* and the *Marquis de Castres*. They anchored off Motuara Island. At first relations between the French and Bay of Islands' Maori were amicable. However it is believed that du Fresne and some of the other Frenchmen violated a tapu—a strict ritual ban—by fishing in Manawaora Bay. The tapu had been placed on the bay after members of a local tribe had drowned there.

Angered by this violation, hundreds of Maori warriors set upon du Fresne and his fishing crew, killing and eating them in an act of utu (vengeance). In retaliation, using their vastly superior cannon and musket firepower, the French killed about 250 Maori.

There is a monument to the memory of Marc-Joseph Marion du Fresne and his compatriots at Te Hue Bay-Assassination Cove, with a plaque summarising the events of 12 June 1772.

There is a walking track around Moturua Island and its interior is a scenic reserve. The bay's largest island, Urupukapuka, has walking tracks, safe sandy beaches for swimming and snorkelling and three public campgrounds.

Most cruises and other excursions depart from Paihia (population 1960), a waterfront town across a bridge just south of Waitangi. Paihia is the main commercial and accommodation centre and tourism hub of the Bay of Islands.

Best-known of the bay's cruises is the 'Cream Trip'. This was begun in 1886 by Albert Fuller, who on his sailing ship *Undine* delivered coal to the islands in the bay. When his vessel became motorised early in the twentieth century, Fuller was able to deliver other supplies to the island communities, as far out as Cape Brett. In 1927 he acquired the 'Cream Trip' route, and his vessel had the facilities to collect cream from the bay's dairy farms. In the 1960s another launch, the *Bay Belle,* took over the Cream Trip run.

Today the *Bay Belle* ferries visitors and locals between Paihia and Russell.

A modern catamaran follows the historic Cream Trip route, which is part of a tourist 'Super Cruise' which takes in the Hole in the Rock and allows a one-hour stopover on Urupukapuka Island. The catamaran leaves Paihia at 10am daily from September to May, and on Monday, Wednesday, Thursday and Saturday during the other months of the year.

Big game fishing is a popular sport in the Bay of Islands. It was first brought to the attention of the outside world in the 1920s by Zane Grey (1879–1939), the famous American writer of western novels (*Riders of the Purple Sage*). Grey regularly visited the area to fish for marlin and other bill fish, tuna and sharks. He dubbed the Bay of Islands 'The angler's El Dorado'.

The Bay of Islands is also New Zealand's most popular yacht cruising destination. It is usually the first port of call for the hundreds of yachts from overseas that drop down from the South Pacific's tropical waters when the cyclone season begins in December. The yachts spend the New Zealand summer sailing on the east coast of Northland until the cyclone season ends in April.

Details of all tours, including boat charters, game fishing and swimming with dolphins, can be obtained from the Bay of islands i-SITE Visitor Centre, the Wharf, Marsden Road, Paihia. Phone: (09) 402 7345. Email: paihia@visitornorthland.co.nz.

Bay of Islands Water Taxi provides fast, on-demand transport to all parts of the bay, including Cape Brett and Moturua Island. Phone: Freephone 0800 387 892; 09 402 5454.

Websites: www.bay-of-islands.co.nz visitboi.co.nz; www.bayofislandsinfo.co.nz; www.waitangi.org.nz; www.exploregroup.com.au/en/amazing-places/bay-of-islands; www.projectislandsong.co.nz.

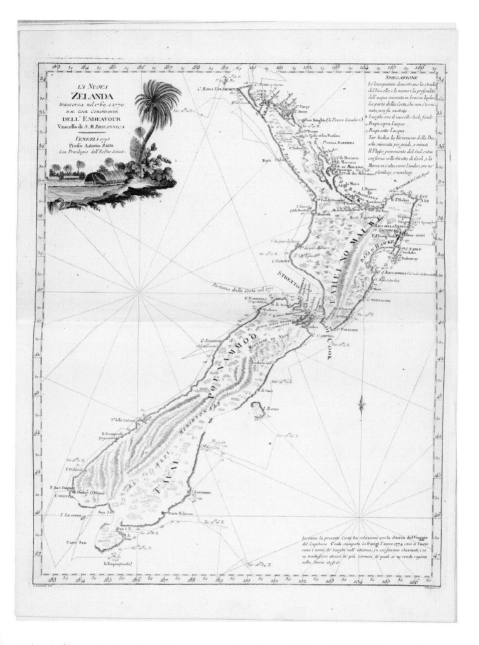

A chart of New Zealand by Italian map-maker Antonio Zatta (1757–97), based on the 1769–70 chart James Cook drew during his first visit to New Zealand. The map shows the course of HMB *Endeavour* around the North and South islands, and for its time is remarkably accurate. The two most glaring errors are that Banks Peninsula is shown as an island and Stewart Island as a peninsula.

Top: Replica of HMB *Endeavour* at sea
Bottom: Replica of HMB *Endeavour* moored at Cairns Wharf, Queensland

Top: James Cook statue by Anthony Stones, Gisborne
Bottom: Turanganui River and Gisborne city

Top: Tauranga Harbour entrance, with a statue of Tangaroa, the
Polynesian God of the Sea (centre)
Bottom: Mural on Mercury Bay Museum, Whitianga

Top: Te Horo Rock, Cathedral Cove, Coromandel
Bottom: The Hole in the Rock, Piercy Island, near Cape Brett, Bay of Islands

Both: The roro, or front of the Maori Meeting House, Waitangi, Bay of Islands

Top: Motukeikei and Motorua Islands, Bay of Islands, viewed from Urapukapuka Island. Roberton-Motuarohia Island to the right, in the distance.
Bottom: Kemp House, Kerikeri

Top: Pompallier House and grounds, Russell, Bay of Islands
Bottom: Kerikeri Basin (foreground), the Stone Store (left) and Kemp House, Kerikeri

HISTORIC RUSSELL

Formerly known as Kororareka, the waterfront town of Russell was the first permanent European settlement and seaport in New Zealand. It began its existence as a supply centre for whaling and sealing ships operating in the South Pacific in the early-nineteenth century. Its harbour provided a safe anchorage and was surrounded by a high population of Maori, who supplied visiting European seamen with food, timber and women. In return Maori sought the Europeans' firearms, alcohol and goods such as clothing and footwear.

In 1842 Jean Baptiste Pompallier established a Roman Catholic mission in Kororareka. The mission house contained a printing press for the production of Maori language religious texts, and a tannery. In 1845 a war was provoked by the repeated felling and re-erecting of the British flag on Flagstaff Hill above Kororareka, by Hone Heke, a local Maori leader. This action was taken as a symbolic protest against British authority in the area. The flagstaff was felled for a fourth time at the beginning of the Battle of Kororareka, during which Heke sacked the town. Its inhabitants fled aboard British ships, which then bombarded what remained of the place with cannon fire.

This tumultuous history contrasts markedly with today's Russell. With a population of just 816, it is a stylish little town of cafes, boutiques, motels, homestays and backpacker hostels. A colonial-era hotel, the Duke of Marlborough, graces the Strand on the waterfront near the centre of the town, and New Zealand's oldest surviving church, Christ Church (1847), stands a little way back from the waterfront, on the corner of Robertson and Baker Streets.

From Maiki Hill in Flagstaff Reserve, above the town to the north, there are panoramic views of the Bay of Islands. On twelve days of the year the flagstaff on the hill flies the original flag of

New Zealand. At the southern end of Russell, Pompallier Mission, the historic printer-tannery-storehouse on the waterfront, has been faithfully restored and is maintained by the New Zealand Historic Places Trust. The Mission building is well worth a visit.

These heritage sites and the town's tranquillity and beachfront location, make visiting Russell a delight. There is also a fine swimming beach, Oneroa Bay, on the other side of the peninsula, a kilometre behind the town.

Russell is reached by road and ferry from SH 11, which branches to the right off SH 1 at Kawakawa town. A vehicle ferry connects Opua, just off SH 11, with the peninsula on which Russell is located. A regular passenger ferry service links Russell with Paihia, directly across the bay. The trip takes fifteen minutes each way.

ENDEAVOUR'S VOYAGE: COOK IN THE BAY OF ISLANDS

Cook and his ship's company were in the Bay of Islands from 29 November until 5 December 1769, with *Endeavour* anchored just south of a small island, Motuarohia. The stay was mainly positive, with much trading between the Endeavours and the bay's Maori population, for fish in particular.

The visit was not without conflict, however. Before they landed on Motuarohia Island Cook observed armed Maori warriors on the shore. Consequently he and the ship's naturalists were accompanied by armed marines when they took the pinnace and yawl and landed on the island. After several hundred warriors advanced on the visitors, Cook's men, greatly outnumbered, fired on them with small shot. A potentially disastrous confrontation was avoided first by the wounding of some of the warriors with the small shot, then more effectively by the firing of a broadside of the ship's cannons. This was ordered by Cook's second-in-command, Zachary Hicks, who was still aboard. The four-pound cannonballs were fired over the heads of the attacking warriors, who retreated rapidly in response to a display of explosive force they had never before experienced.

Relieved from the threat of attack, Cook's party rowed to another beach on the island, disembarked and climbed a hill, from where there were fine views of the bay. Hence Banks's admiring description, as quoted earlier.

Thereafter relations with the Maori were mainly peaceful. The bay's natural features were recorded in the journals, charts and drawings of Cook and his naturalists. Sydney Parkinson and Herman Sporing drew detailed profiles of Motuarohia Island. Sporing's drawing of the eastern headland of Motuarohia clearly illustrates the features of a palisaded pa, referred to by *Endeavour*'s scientists as a 'Hippa', an English interpretation of the Maori name 'He-pa'. Cook and the others observed large quantities of fish being caught by the local people, using very long nets made from woven strips of flax.

The Endeavours were also able to become acquainted with the islands between Tapeka Point, a peninsula which extends into the bay from its southern shore, and Cape Brett to the east. These islands are Motuarohia, Moturua,

Motukiekie and Urupukapuka. Today Motuarohia is also referred to as Roberton Island, as well as by its original, official name. As there was little fresh water on Motuarohia, Cook and his men obtained fresh supplies from a stream at Waipao Bay, on larger Moturua Island.

On 4 December Cook and the naturalists were rowed over to the mainland. On the way they passed a headland upon which was a pa, and its inhabitants invited them ashore. The site was probably on the Okawa Peninsula. Here the visitors were shown large gardens where kumara and yams were being cultivated, and more to their surprise, paper mulberry trees. From the bark of these trees the local Maori made cloth, in the same manner as Cook, Banks and the others had observed it being made on Tahiti earlier that year.

The departure of *Endeavour* from the Bay of Islands on 5 December was not straightforward. At first the ship was becalmed, then after darkness she was driven by a current close to one of the islands. Misfortune was averted by the vessel being towed clear by one of her boats, assisted by light air springing up from the south. No sooner had this happened when the ship struck a rock on the outer margin of the bay. Fortunately the rock was to windward of the ship, and she was able to free herself from it without damage to the hull. Cook called the rock Whale Rock; Maori knew it as Te Nunuhe.

Now free from danger, *Endeavour* was again in open sea and on 6 December she resumed a northward course.

THE *RAINBOW WARRIOR* DIVE SITE

On 10 July 1985 an act of international terrorism occurred in New Zealand. That night French saboteurs attached two limpet mines to the hull of the *Rainbow Warrior,* the Greenpeace flagship, while she was moored at a wharf in the port of Auckland. The vessel was preparing to sail to Moruroa atoll, in French Polynesia, to protest against a planned nuclear test on the island. A photographer on the *Rainbow Warrior,* Fernando Pereira, drowned when it sank.

Although most of the French saboteurs fled the country, two military agents, Captain Dominique Prieur and Commander Alain Mafart, were captured by the New Zealand Police and charged with manslaughter. Convicted and sentenced to ten years in prison, they were subsequently transferred to Hao atoll in French Polynesia before shortly afterwards being freed by the French authorities.

Matauri Bay is on the east coast of Northland, 30 kilometres north of Kerikeri. The bay has a white sand beach, very clear water, and is a popular site for campers and other holidaymakers. The Cavalli Islands lie north-east of Matauri Bay, a group of several small islands and a much larger one, Motukawanui.

Matauri Bay is also the last resting place of the *Rainbow Warrior.* After its hull was patched to cover the gash inflicted by the French saboteurs' mines, the ship was towed north, in December 1987. It was accorded a traditional Maori burial, then scuttled in Matauri Bay. The ship's masts had been removed and sent to the museum at Dargaville, on the Wairoa River.

Since its sinking in the crystal-clear waters of Matauri Bay, the *Rainbow Warrior* has become a living reef, attracting a rich marine life. In this way the ship's remains have become an integral part of the marine environment the vessel's original existence was intended to help protect. Covered in invertebrate life, the *Rainbow Warrior* has become a haven for schooling fish and one of New Zealand's most popular dive sites, attracting scuba divers from all over the world.

A striking memorial to the *Rainbow Warrior* by environmental artist Chris Booth stands on a hill above Matauri Bay. From the site there are majestic views of Matauri Bay and the Cavalli Islands.

The Twin Coast Discovery Highway

This road touring route is circular, starting and ending at Auckland. Approximately 200 kilometres long, the highway incorporates both coasts of Northland, with the Tasman Sea to the west and the Pacific Ocean to the east. During his circumnavigation of New Zealand in 1769-70, James Cook sailed along both these shores, going north along the Pacific coast and south down the Tasman coast. Along the Twin Coast Discovery Highway are lovely beaches, harbours, historic sites and centres of marine activity.

Beginning with the eastern coast, the highway takes in the seaside town of Orewa, which fronts a very long beach, then continues north to Waiwera, where there is a complex of thermal swimming pools. The attractive riverside town of Warkworth is a half-hour drive further on, just off SH 1.

Whangarei (86,000) is Northland's only city and a hub for visitors. It has art galleries and working craft studios and a Town Basin where cruising vessels from many countries are moored. There are several walking tracks on Bream Head, while north-east of Whangarei is Tutukaka, a fishing and diving base with daily excursions to the dive sites of the Poor Knights islands.

The Bay of Islands offers a great variety of marine recreational activities, Russell has several important heritage buildings, while Paihia across the bay is a tourist excursion and accommodation centre for the bay. Nearby Waitangi, Kerikeri and Waimate North have strong associations with New Zealand's colonial past.

Heading inland from the Bay of Islands the Twin Coast Discovery Highway passes through stands of native forest before emerging on the west coast near the town of Kaitaia. From here it's possible to head to the far north and Cape Reinga, or turn south to Rawene town, on the southern shore of the tranquil Hokianga Harbour. There are several art galleries and craft boutiques in Rawene.

Further south on the west coast, SH 12 passes along the Kauri Coast. A highlight here is the Waipoua Forest, home of the world's tallest kauri tree, awe-inspiring Tane Mahuta. The highway passes through the town of Dargaville (4251) on the Wairoa River, which flows into the huge Kaipara Harbour.

The highway proceeds south to Ruawai. There SH 12 turns east and passes through the little settlement of Matakohe. Here the excellent Kauri Museum has exhibits displaying the history of the Kaipara region, timber milling in particular.

SH 12 continues east to Brynderwyn, where it joins SH 1. After turning right here, the Discovery Highway goes directly south to Auckland on SH 1.

Website: www.fourcorners.co.nz/new-zealand/twin-coast-discovery.

ENDEAVOUR'S VOYAGE: TO THE FAR NORTH

Christmas 1769–New Year 1770

After battling gale-force winds off the north-east coast of the North Island, in mid-December 1769 *Endeavour* doubled the island's northernmost point. In spite of the unfavourable weather, Cook named North Cape and fixed its position accurately. Christmas Day was celebrated in the vicinity of the Three Kings Islands, to the north, which had been named by Abel Tasman early in 1643.

During a lull in the stormy conditions Joseph Banks shot several gannets and they were dressed and baked into a pie for the *Endeavour*'s Christmas dinner. Banks recorded the celebration as follows, 'Our Goose pye was eat with great approbation and in the Evening all hands were as Drunk as our forefathers usd to be upon the like occasion.'[4]

The following day he noted, ruefully, 'This morn all heads ached with yesterday's debauch'.

CAPE REINGA

The Far North of New Zealand is a magical place. The North Island tapers away, narrowing at the Aupouri Peninsula, then broadening to a knuckle of land that culminates in its extremity, North Cape, and further west, Cape Reinga. Off these capes, two great bodies of water meet—the Tasman Sea and the Pacific Ocean. There is a lighthouse on Cape Reinga, and from its elevated site the turbulence created by the meeting of the two seas can be clearly seen. It is an awe-inspiring sight. To the right, below the cape, is the wide scoop of Spirits Bay-Piwhane.

Cape Reinga has great spiritual significance to Maori. Its full name is 'Cape Reinga-Te Rerenga Wairua', which means 'Leaping-off Place of Spirits'. Traditional Maori belief holds that the cape marks the place where the spirits of the dead enter the underworld before their return to the traditional Polynesian homeland, Hawaiiki. The spirits turn briefly at Three Kings Islands, for one last look back towards the mainland, before resuming the journey to their spiritual home.

SH 1, now sealed all the way, proceeds up the middle of the Aupouri Peninsula to Cape Reinga. The cape is a very popular tourist destination, receiving over 120,000 visitors a year. It is not possible to access North Cape by public road. One-day coach tours to Cape Reinga can be taken. Most leave from the Far North's main town, Kaitaia, or Paihia in the Bay of Islands. The coaches drive along Ninety Mile Beach (actually 56 miles/90 kilometres long), on the western side of the peninsula, then access the cape by a side road. Taking one of these tours is highly recommended.

For accommodation, attractions and activities in the Far North, refer to Far North i-Site Visitor Centre, Te Ahu, cnr Matthews Avenue and South Road, Kaitaia. Phone (09) 408 9450. Email kaitaia@visitnorthland.co.nz. Website: northlandnz.com.

Mount Taranaki

CHAPTER FIVE

NORTH ISLAND WEST COAST

...the prevailing Westerly winds impel upon the Shore must render this a very Dangerous Coast.

ENDEAVOUR'S VOYAGE: THE WEST COAST OF THE NORTH ISLAND

After sailing around the extreme north of New Zealand, Cook took *Endeavour* west, around Cape Maria van Diemen (also named by Abel Tasman) and during the New Year, 1770, down the west coast of the North Island.

The west coast is very different to the east coast of the North Island. Instead of island groups, estuaries, sheltered bays and inlets, the west coast has long expanses of exposed land, sand dunes and cliffs. Strong swells are constant, the few harbours have narrow entrances and the prevailing south-west winds make entering them hazardous.

Consequently Cook was obliged to keep *Endeavour* well off this lee shore. He noted in his journal:

The great sea which the prevailing westerly winds impel upon the Shore must render this a very dangerous coast, this I am so fully sencible of that once clear of it I am determind not to come so near again if I can possible avoide it unless we have a very favourable wind indeed.[2]

So, no landings were made, although by 7 January the winds had abated, allowing *Endeavour* to sail closer to the coast. On 10 January they passed the entrance to Raglan Harbour, at 37° 48' South latitude, and passed an island covered in sea birds. Cook named it 'Gannet Island'.

Continuing south, on the evening of 12 January the Endeavours saw on the southern horizon the peak of a very high mountain. At dawn three days later they saw, in Cook's words, 'For a few Minutes the Top of the peaked Mountain above the Clowds, bearing NE, it is of a prodigious height and its top is cover'd with everlasting snow.'[2]

Banks, Parkinson and the others were impressed by the spectacular landmark. Banks described it as 'certainly the noblest hill I have ever seen.' Cook named it 'Mount Egmont', after John Perceval, second Earl of Egmont and First Lord of the Admiralty from 1763 to 1766, and a supporter of the search for the Great Unknown Southern Continent. Cook also named the westernmost extremity of the North Island, 'Cape Egmont'.

Two years later, in March 1772, French navigator Marc-Joseph Marion du Fresne was off the same coast. Unaware of Cook's earlier visit, he named the mountain 'Pic Mascarin' after one of his two ships. The French name didn't stick. 'Egmont' did, until it was replaced by 'Taranaki' in the 1980s.

MOUNT TARANAKI

In 1986 the Minister of Lands in New Zealand decreed that the mountain that looms over Taranaki province and which Cook named 'Mt Egmont' would henceforth have an official alternative and equal name, 'Mount Taranaki'. For centuries local Maori had known the mountain as 'Taranaki', a name derived from 'tara' meaning peak and 'naki' (from 'ngaki') meaning shining. Even in mid-summer, when Cook saw the mountain, the summit usually has a covering of snow, hence the adjective 'shining'.

According to Maori mythology, Taranaki mountain once lived in the centre of the North Island, alongside a trio of other volcanoes, Ruapehu, Tongariro and Ngauruhoe. A beautiful maiden, Pihanga, was desired by all the mountains, and a great battle was fought for her favours. It was won by Tongariro, who in the process wounded Taranaki grievously. He then fled to the west, creating deep gorges along the way. These were filled by the Whanganui River, which rises on the slopes of Mt Ruapehu. Now, when Mt Taranaki hides himself with rainclouds, he is said to be weeping for his lost love. And when spectacular sunsets illuminate the mountain's slopes, Taranaki is said to be presenting himself to her.

Mount Taranaki is a dormant volcano, 2518 metres high. Its coordinates are 39° 17' South latitude and 174° 03' East longitude. There is a secondary cone, named Fantham's Peak and known to Maori as Panitahi, on the south side of the mountain. Mt Taranaki's conic symmetry has seen it compared to Japan's Mount

Fujiyama, and indeed it provided the backdrop for the movie *The Last Samurai* (2003), starring Tom Cruise.

The last major eruption of Mt Taranaki occurred in about 1755, fourteen years before James Cook sighted it. There have also been minor eruptions since then within the crater, the latest in 1854. Around the ring plain of the mountain are many 'lahars', mounds resulting from eruptions. These are particularly noticeable on the farmland on the mountain's western side, inland from Cape Egmont.

Other volcanic landforms in Taranaki province are the Pouakai Ranges, to the west of the mountain, and Paritutu Rock (156 metres) and the Sugar Loaf Islands, just off-shore near Port Taranaki. These islands were also named by Cook when he passed them in *Endeavour*. Today the Sugar Loaves and the surrounding sea are a maritime park.

Mt Taranaki is popular with alpine climbers and tramping clubs. The peak was first climbed by Europeans in 1839, by naturalist Ernst Dieffenbach and James Heberly. Their ascent of the mountain is recreated in the novel *The Naturalist,* by Thom Conroy (Vintage, 2014).

Today in Taranaki a circular area with a radius of 9.6 kilometres from the mountain's summit is maintained as a forest reserve, called Egmont National Park. This protected zone is covered in native forest, mostly northern rata and rimu. The forested zone differentiates sharply from the pastureland below it. Like most of Taranaki province, the farmland is devoted to dairying.

An ascent of Mount Taranaki appears straightforward. This is deceptive. The mountain has incurred a high casualty rate over the last century and a half, mainly because weather conditions on its slopes can change with unexpected speed. Since records began in 1891, 83 people have died on the mountain.

There are three roads leading part of the way up Mt Taranaki. The highest of these is to East Egmont plateau, which is reached via a turn-off from SH 3, at the town of Stratford. From Stratford the eastern side road leads to the Mountain House and Mount Taranaki's small ski field. There are park visitor centres at North Egmont, reached from a turn-off from SH 3 at Egmont Village, and at Dawson Falls on the south-east side of the mountain. Dawson Falls is reached via Kaponga, a small settlement west of the town of Eltham. There is no road access to the mountain from the western side, although there are tramping tracks and huts in the vicinity.

The capital of Taranaki is New Plymouth (56,300). A coastal city and port, the town was founded by English immigrants in the 1840s, mainly from the county of Devon. New Plymouth's long main thoroughfare is called Devon Street. There is another James Cook connection with Taranaki in that the port of Plymouth in England was the departure point for all three of his world voyages.

A ten-kilometre-long walkway, the New Plymouth Coastal Walkway, extends from near Port Taranaki to Bell Block, east of New Plymouth. The walkway affords views of the Tasman Sea, Mt Taranaki, Paritutu Rock and the Sugarloaf Islands.

James Cook's naming rites

Cook no doubt enjoyed giving names to the physical features of the New Zealand coastline he came upon. He was probably aware that the names he gave them would endure on future maps of the country. Most of Cook's names have lasted, although many of the landforms are now bracketed with their Maori nomenclature, which predated Cook's by many years.

111

So, how did Cook decide what to name the landmarks he came across on *Endeavour* and, later, on *Resolution*?

In various ways.

Sometimes he named landforms after eminent people in England whom Cook knew and admired. These eponymous features include Cape Palliser, near the entrance to Wellington Harbour, named after Cook's naval friend and supporter, Hugh Palliser (1722-1796). Stephen's Island and Cape Stephens, in Cook Strait, were named after Sir Philip Stephens (1725-1809), secretary to the Admiralty. Hawke Bay honoured Lord Hawke (1710-1781), a distinguished English naval commander, and Queen Charlotte Sound was named after King George III's wife, Charlotte of Mecklenburg-Strelitz, Queen of Great Britain and Ireland.

Cape Colville was named after Alexander Colvill, 7th Baron Colvill (1717-1770), also a Royal Navy commander, and Cape Jackson in the Marlborough Sounds honoured Sir George Jackson (1725-1822), assistant secretary to the Lords Commissioners of the Admiralty. Port Jackson, the future site of Sydney, Australia, was also named after this man. Cape (sometimes known as Point) Rodney, on the east coast of Northland, Cook named after George Brydges Rodney (1718-1792), 1st Baron Rodney, an English naval hero and a prominent officer in the Royal Navy in Cook's time.

Cook named a cape of the east coast of Northland 'Cape Brett', after Sir Piercy Brett, one of the Lords of the Admiralty who had issued the Instructions for the *Endeavour* voyage. In an unusually quirky gesture, Cook named an island just off Cape Brett, 'Piercy Island' because the island is 'pierced' by a hole.

Other features Cook named for their geographic prominence. For example, East Cape, the Bay of Plenty, North Cape, the Bay of Islands, Great and Little Barrier Islands. The latter pair, Cook found, provided a welcome barrier between the Hauraki Gulf and the Pacific Ocean.

Some features commemorate an important event which occurred during Cook's circumnavigation of New Zealand. For example, Cannibal Cove, Cape Foulwind, Farewell Spit and Cape Farewell.

If a place bore a definite resemblance to a place he knew in England, Cook applied the name to its New Zealand counterpart. For instance he named the wide body of water adjacent to the western Coromandel Peninsula the 'Firth of Thames', and the large river that flowed into it, the 'Thames', after London's great river. Portland Island in northern Hawkes Bay was named after Portland Island in county Dorset, England.

Occasionally Cook named places after the ships that had faithfully taken him around the world. In New Zealand both HMS *Endeavour* and HMS *Resolution* gave their names to Endeavour Inlet and Resolution Bay, in Queen Charlotte Sound.*

Although not as a rule given to metaphorical flourishes, Cook did sometimes name features for their physical resemblance to people or creatures. Thus Mayor Island was followed by the neighbouring Aldermen Islands. Further north, the Hen and Chickens Islands and the Poor Knights group are metaphorical, the latter islands said to resemble an English, potato-based pudding. The hump of Mt Camel, in Northland, is also figurative, as is Five Fingers Point, near the entrance to Dusky Sound.

People aboard Cook's ships were occasionally honoured. Zachary Hicks, afflicted with tuberculosis aboard *Endeavour*, is commemorated by Hicks Bay, in Eastland, and Robert Cooper and Richard Pickersgill, officers aboard *Resolution*, have features in Dusky Sound named after them. There is also a Pickersgill Island in Queen Charlotte Sound. It is thought that Mt Edgecumbe, a volcanic cone in the Bay of Plenty, was named after John Edgecumbe, the sergeant of marines aboard *Endeavour*. The lad Nicholas Young, who first sighted the land of New Zealand from *Endeavour*'s masthead, is immortalised by Young Nicks Head, off the coast of Poverty Bay.

The redoubtable Joseph Banks gave his name to one of the South Island's most prominent features, volcanic Banks Peninsula (although it was mistaken for an island at the time), and it's said that Banks himself suggested that the formidable body of water separating the North and South Islands of New Zealand be named 'Cook Strait'.

*HMB *Endeavour* also lent its name to the Endeavour Strait and the Endeavour River, both in Queensland, Australia. Resolution Cove, in Nootka Sound, Canada, and Port Resolution, on Tanna Island in Vanuatu, were named after Cook's HMS *Resolution*.

COOK PLACENAMES IN THE NORTH ISLAND – TE IKA A MAUI

Poverty Bay, Hawke Bay, Cape Kidnappers, Cape Turnagain, Bare Island, Portland Island, Young Nicks Head, East Cape, Cape Runaway, Hicks Bay, Midway Point, Mt Edgecumbe, Bay of Plenty, White Island, Mayor Island, Castle Island, Alderman Islands, Slipper Island, Mercury Bay, Shakespeare Cliff, Mercury Islands, Cape Colville, Firth of Thames, Little Barrier Island, Great Barrier Island, Hen and Chickens Islands, Bream Tail, Bream Bay, Bream Head, Poor Knights Islands, Cape Brett, Piercy Island, Cavalli Islands, Bay of Islands, Doubtless Bay, Mt Camel, North Cape, Gannet Island, Mt Egmont, Sugar Loaf islands, Cape Egmont, Cape Palliser.

COOK PLACENAMES IN THE SOUTH ISLAND – TE WAI POUNAMU

Admiralty Bay, Queen Charlotte Sound, Cape Jackson, Port Gore, Cannibal Cove, Cloudy Bay, Stephens Island, Cape Stephens, Banks Peninsula, Dusky Sound, Five Fingers Point, Resolution Island, Anchor Island, Wet Jacket Arm, Cooper Island, Pickersgill Harbour, Supper Cove, Luncheon Cove, Breaksea Sound, Doubtful Sound, Cape Foulwind, Farewell Spit, Cape Farewell.

West Head, entrance to Tory Channel

CHAPTER SIX

THE MARLBOROUGH SOUNDS

At 2oClock we Anchor'd in a very snug Cove…

The Marlborough Sounds, of which Queen Charlotte Sound is the largest, occupy the north-eastern corner of the South Island of New Zealand. They consist of a complex of drowned river valleys, caused by tectonic movements that led to a tilting of the Earth's crust to the north-east. The resultant flooding of the river valleys created a labyrinth of waterways and a fretwork of peninsulas, islands, inlets and promontories, most of which open out onto Cook Strait.

The Marlborough Sounds comprise one of the most picturesque regions of New Zealand. The sheltered waterways are ideal for swimming, boating, sailing, fishing and diving. Dolphins, little blue penguins and fur seals are often seen in the sounds. Some parts provide a location for intensive aquaculture—salmon and mussel farming.

The sounds is a region where the boat replaces the motor vehicle as the principal means of transportation and communication. Many of the outer reaches of the sounds, such as Ship Cove, are accessible only by walking tracks or the sea. Scheduled tours of the sounds

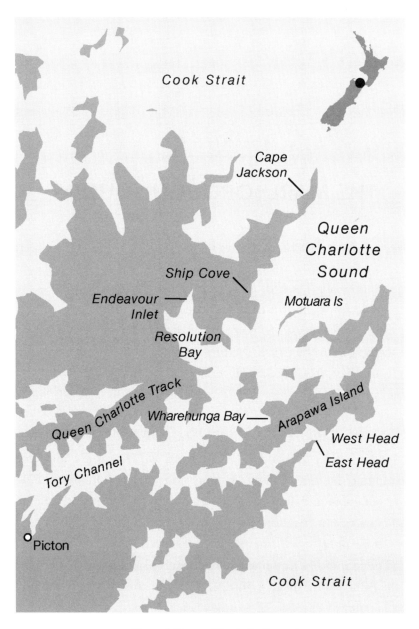

Map of Queen Charlotte Sound

can be taken from Picton, and water taxis are available for reaching the remoter bays. There are a number of deluxe holiday resorts throughout the sounds.

Plan and book via the website: www.MarlboroughNZ.com.

ENDEAVOUR'S VOYAGE: QUEEN CHARLOTTE SOUND

By mid-January 1770, sailing towards the southernmost point of the North Island, Cook was anxious to find a sheltered anchorage for *Endeavour*. It was six months since the ship had left Matavai Bay, and her sailing speed was being hampered by the weeds and crustaceans attached to her hull. The ship needed to be careened and scrubbed, and repairs made to her sails, spars and rigging. Also, after the arduous doubling of North Cape and the continuous sail down the west coast of the North Island, supplies of fresh food, water and wood were needed.

At dawn on 15 January *Endeavour* entered a wide bay, not far from where Tasman had had a fatal altercation with Maori in December 1642. Unaware that the 'bay' would eventually prove to be a strait separating the two largest islands of New Zealand, *Endeavour* sailed further east for about eleven kilometres. The bay became a channel. The land on both sides at first appeared barren, then further into the channel it became forested.

At noon that same day *Endeavour* came to a long narrow island near the centre of the channel. The ship was towed by her boats around the island's south-western point, on which a fortified village had been built. Cook again referred to this as a 'Hippa', similar to the one he had observed on a point of Motuarohia Island, in the Bay of Islands. The main island was inhabited, and the natives on it shouted defiance and waved weapons at *Endeavour*, the huge, outlandish vaka which had entered their domain. Cook later learned that Maori called the island 'Motuara', which means 'Island in the Path', and that the strait surrounding it was 'Totara-Nui', meaning 'Big Totara' [trees].

Endeavour was towed a couple of miles due west of Motuara, to a sheltered cove. Here the stream anchor was lowered in eleven fathoms of water. Cook named the place 'Ship Cove'; Maori called it 'Mere-Toto'.

This January 1770 stopover was the first of Cook's five visits to Ship Cove, which became his favourite anchorage in New Zealand. Here he repaired and provisioned his ships before sailing on to the tropical South Pacific.

During the first visit Cook and *Endeavour* stayed at Ship Cove from 15 January until 6 February, 1770. On subsequent visits to the cove he was in command of HMS *Resolution*. He anchored *Resolution* here from 18 May until 7 June 1773, from 3 November until 25 November 1773, from 18 October until 10 November 1774 and finally from 12 February until 25 February, 1777. During this final stopover *Resolution*'s consort vessel was HMS *Discovery*, commanded by Charles Clerke. The earlier consort vessel to *Resolution* was HMS *Adventure*, captained by Tobias Furneaux.

Ship Cove and Motuara Island are on the western side of Queen Charlotte Sound. The cove is overlooked by steep, forested hills in which a clear stream rises, then flows down into the sound. The swift descent of the water made the filling of Cook's ships' water casks a little easier. The beauty of the cove enchanted Cook's men. Banks in particular appreciated the loveliness of the birdsong emanating from the surrounding forest. It resonated with the melodious calls of bellbirds, saddleback, huia and kokako.

The visiting ships' artists and illustrators: Sydney Parkinson (first voyage to Ship Cove on *Endeavour*) William Hodges (second voyage on *Resolution*), Johann and George Forster (second voyage on *Resolution*), and John Webber (third voyage on *Resolution* and her final visit) found plenty of human and botanical interest to depict in their drawings.

During Cook's first, three-week stay at Ship Cove the little bay and its environs supplied almost everything that the *Endeavour* expedition required: fresh water from the stream, wood from the forest for the galley and timber for replacement spars, plentiful fish and shellfish, 'scurvy grass' as an anti-scorbutic and fodder for the ship's animals. The area surrounding the cove was well suited to hunting and gathering. The crew shot and roasted shags, collected mussels and oysters from the rocks and seined for fish. One day *Endeavour*'s men hauled in 135 kilograms of fish, including tarakihi, mullet, mackerel and blue cod. Cook and Banks also observed the skilled fish netting techniques of the local Maori.

Maori on Motuara Island, after their initial hostility, were welcoming and willing to trade. Communications with them were made easier by the presence on *Endeavour* of the Society Islands' priest-navigator, Tupaia, who had come aboard the ship at Tahiti. His language was very similar to that of the New Zealand Maori. He, Cook and his officers became friends with a Motuara chief, an elderly man called Topaa.

Cook and the others explored the sound. At a bay a little north of Ship Cove he, Banks and Tupaia came upon the unmistakeable remains of a recent feast of human body parts. This confirmed what European people had suspected, that Maori practised anthropophagy, or cannibalism. The Englishmen promptly named the place 'Cannibal Cove'. The Maori of Motuara Island later traded human bones for Tahitian cloth with *Endeavour*'s crew.

Cook climbed to the summit of an island to the south of Ship Cove and observed that the great strait joined the western to the eastern sea, the Tasman Sea to the Pacific Ocean. Maori knew the formidable strait as 'Raukawa-Moana'; it is said to have been named 'Cook Strait' by Joseph Banks

Cook climbed to the highest point of Motuara Island, had a post set up there, hoisted the English flag upon it and took possession of the sound and its surrounding region for England. He also climbed a hill near Cape Jackson and had built upon it a cairn, in which he placed a silver coin, beads and musket balls.

Cook and his ship's company became aware that

Motuara Island was a place of refuge for the local Maori, who consisted mainly of kinship groups. Cook also noted that the people in this area did not seem nearly as prosperous as those they had met in the North Island. They also seemed insecure and apprehensive. This was probably because the people of Totara Nui-Queen Charlotte Sound were often under threat of attack from war parties from the North Island. Life around the sound was uncertain because of these raids, which were usually carried out by parties on their way south to procure the prized greenstone of the west coast of Te Wai Pounamu (the South Island).

PICTON

The principal town serving the Marlborough Sounds is Picton (4300), which lies at the head of Queen Charlotte Sound. Surrounded on both sides by hills, the town was formerly a whaling station. Today it is a port, a tourist hub and the South Island's railhead. Its sheltered location means that it is a base for pleasure craft and charter boats, as well as for the arrival and departure point of the ferries that cross Cook Strait, to and from Wellington. There is a large pleasure boat marina in Picton harbour and another at Waikawa Bay, just north-east of the town.

Small planes link Wellington to Picton Airport, five kilometres south of the town. There is a much larger airport at Blenheim, twenty minutes by road south of Picton. Scheduled flights from Auckland, Wellington and Christchurch fly in and out of Blenheim airport.

Two ferry companies serve the Cook Strait route, with several sailings daily. The voyage across the strait takes approximately three hours each way, and the ferries accommodate vehicles as well as passengers. Part of the sea journey takes the ferries into Queen

Charlotte Sound via Tory Channel, a gateway to Cook Strait. Picton is also an increasingly popular port of call for cruise liners, especially in the summer months.

If coming to Picton by car from Christchurch, the drive along the east coast on SH 1, via Kaikoura, is one of the most scenic in New Zealand. It is also possible to travel from Christchurch to Picton by the Coastal Pacific train, which for much of the journey runs alongside the sea. The train travel time from Christchurch is five hours, fifteen minutes.*

SH 1 becomes Auckland Street when it passes just to the west of Picton's central business district. Auckland Street runs parallel to the town's main north–south thoroughfare, High Street. London Quay branches to the right from High Street, at the lower end of the town. From London Quay there are views of the waterfront reserve and Picton Harbour. Several cafes enable the patrons to enjoy these views.

One of the London Quay cafes, Seabreeze, features a small display of James Cook memorabilia. There is a large map of Queen Charlotte Sound on one wall, and among the offerings on the Seabreeze menu are 'Captain Cook Fishcakes'.

One of the central Picton cafes makes an excellent refreshment stop if exploring the town's waterfront on foot. London Quay also has a number of quality souvenir boutiques.

Close to the Picton marina, near the junction of Wellington Street and Waikawa Road, are a number of hotels and motels. These are only a few minutes' walk from Picton's waterfront reserve and central business district. James Cook's ship and his Queen are commemorated by Endeavour Park, which is next to Queen Charlotte College, in Waikawa Road.

London Quay overlooks a waterfront reserve, where there is a children's playground and an aquarium. The Picton Museum is located above the reserve, and features exhibits depicting the town's whaling and pioneering history. The National Whale Centre Display and Development Hub is also located on Picton's waterfront, and every January the Picton Maritime Festival, a free event, is held on the reserve. A short walk to the north-west, at Dunbar Wharf, is the Edwin Fox Museum. The *Edwin Fox* is the world's second oldest surviving merchant sailing ship and the only one still in existence from Australia's convict transportation era.

Charter boats depart daily from Picton wharf for day tours of Queen Charlotte Sound. Two companies, Beachcomber Cruises 'Magic Mail Run' and the Cougar Line run daily launch trips from the wharf to the beginning of the Queen Charlotte Track, and to Ship Cove and Motuara Island Bird Sanctuary. Ship Cove, James Cook's base during his stays at Queen Charlotte Sound, is an hour away by launch from Picton Harbour. Motuara Island is 45–50 minutes from Picton Harbour.

Picton Water Taxis provide on demand, fast transport to outlying parts of Queen Charlotte Sound. Phone 03 573 7853.

Beachcomber Cruises Picton: cruises to all parts of Queen Charlotte Sound. Phone: Freephone 0800 624 526.

Email office@mailboat.co.nz.

* A powerful earthquake, measuring 7.8 on the Richter scale, struck this area just after midnight on 14 November 2016. The 'quake, which was centred in north Canterbury, brought several large landslides down on SH 1 and the Main Trunk railway line. Kaikoura town was cut off from the rest of the South Island for days. Although only two people

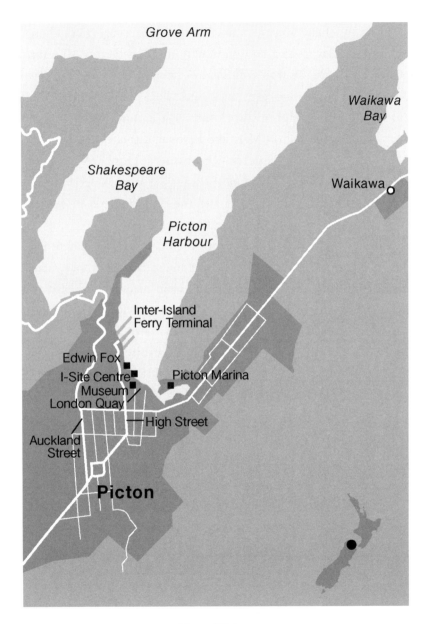

Map of Picton

were killed by the 'quake, there was severe damage to homes and major disruption to the East Coast Highway and the rail line from Christchurch to Picton. Repairs to the highway and rail line took many months.

Picton's Snout Walking Track & Waikawa Bay

The Snout Walking Track follows the western shoreline of a high peninsula that separates Picton Harbour from Waikawa Bay. The track provides great views of the harbour and sound. Begin the track by crossing the 'Coathanger Bridge' across the Picton marina, then continue walking to Shelley Beach. From there the track goes on to the Queen Charlotte View lookout, then proceeds to a picnic area at the end of the headland.

The walk takes about 90 minutes each way. It is 50 minutes to Queen Charlotte View, then another 40 minutes to Snout Head itself.

Driving from central Picton to Waikawa Bay takes about ten minutes. Sitting on the reserve above the beach at Waikawa Bay and savouring the outlook across the water is the perfect location for a fish-and-chip meal. The fish should be South Island blue cod, accompanied by a chilled sauvignon blanc from one of the many Marlborough wineries. A half hour drive south of Picton, Marlborough is New Zealand's largest grape-growing region, famous for its sauvignon blanc.

MOTUARA ISLAND

Motuara Island played a significant part in James Cook's stopovers in Queen Charlotte Sound. When *Endeavour* arrived in the sound for the first time, in January 1770, the promontory at the southern end of Motuara Island was occupied by a Maori village. Cook called this 'Hip-pa Island' after the Maori word 'pa'. The steepness of the headland's slopes made palisade fortifications unnecessary. Cook and the others closely noted the construction of Maori houses and other buildings while visiting this pa.

The main island of Motuara has two peaks. The northern peak is about two metres higher than the southern peak, which is 120 metres above sea level. On 31 January Cook 1770 raised the British flag on the southern peak of the island and took formal possession of the whole of Te Wai Pounamu—the South Island of New Zealand—for his sovereign, King George III.

On his second stopover in the sound in 1773, following a directive from George III, who was also known as 'Farmer George', Cook made serious attempts to introduce English seeds and plants to Motuara Island. He planted potatoes, corn, beans, carrots and parsnips, and instructed local Maori as to how the plants should be nurtured.

Over 130 years later, during the early 1900s, most of Motuara Island's trees were felled and the cleared land was planted in pasture. A photograph taken of the island's summit in 1902 shows a ravaged landscape of tree stumps, with pastureland between them. In 1920 a cairn was erected on the site where Cook claimed Queen Charlotte Sound and 'the adjacent lands' for King George III. The cairn is still there.

Over the last 25 years the landscape of Motuara Island has been transformed. The island is now a wildlife refuge, administered by New Zealand's Department of Conservation. All introduced pests such as opossums, rats and stoats have been eradicated from the island. Consequently its native forest has regenerated. Indigenous fauna and flora now thrive, with several bird species critically endangered on the mainland being protected on predator-free Motuara.

Top: View from the wharf, Russell, Bay of Islands
Bottom: The waterfront at Russell

Top: Motuara Island from above Ship Cove
Bottom: Ship Cove

Top: East Head, entrance to Tory Channel
Bottom: Cook Monument, Ship Cove

Top: Waterfall, Dusky Sound
Bottom: Dusky Sound, looking east to the Southern Alps

Top: Cook Monument, Ship Cove
Bottom: The Seaforth River flows into Dusky Sound at Supper Cover

Top: Sunset over the Marlborough Sounds, from the Kapiti Coast
Bottom: Astronomer's Point, Pickersgill Harbour, Dusky Sound

Top: Supper Cove trampers' hut, Dusky Sound
Bottom: Late afternoon light, Dusky Sound

Top: Fur Seal rookery, Dusky Sound
Bottom left: Fur Seal, Dusky Sound. Bottom right: Dusky Sound penguin.

This birdlife includes the saddleback (tieke), the New Zealand robin (toutouwai), bellbird (korimako), tui, grey warbler (riroriro), bush pigeon (kereru), silvereye (tauhou), fantail (piwakawaka), the endangered South Island saddleback and the very rare king shag. Little Blue penguins nest on the island, and the Maud Island frog and the Marlborough green gecko also make the place their home. In this way Motuara is in a healthier environmental state than it was when James Cook and men visited the island in the 1770s.

There is a jetty on the south-western side of Motuara. From the jetty a track winds up through the regenerating forest to the island's highest point. From the summit there are views over to Ship Cove and right across Queen Charlotte Sound.

Beachcomber Cruises operate launches which take visitors to Motuara Island daily. The half-day trip departs at 7.30am daily from Picton Wharf. This allows for one hour on the island. There are no toilets or facilities for the disabled on Motuara, although there are toilets on board the launches.

Arrival time back in Picton is 12.30pm.

The inter-island ferries

The most memorable means of entering or leaving Queen Charlotte Sound is on board one of the inter-island ferries that connect Picton and Wellington. The ferry route includes a half hour of sailing into or out of Picton harbour, and from the decks of the ferry there are spellbinding views of the sound and its islands.

The ferries enter or leave Queen Charlotte Sound through a narrow opening from Cook Strait. This pass is between two rocky headlands, East Head and West Head. It then opens out into Tory Channel. For the first or last half hour of the voyage passengers can enjoy the unique scenery of the channel and the wider sound.

On their way through the sound the ferries glide past farmland, holiday cottages, pine plantations, salmon farms and small coves, each one with its own jetty. There are always launches and yachts to observe in the sound from the ferry decks, some of the hundreds that moor at Picton or Waikawa Bay. As the ferry swings around the southern end of Arapawa Island and enters Queen Charlotte Sound proper, there are views to the north-east, towards the islands that Cook knew well, including Motuara.

Two ferry companies service the Cook Strait crossing, Bluebridge and the Interislander. There are several sailings per day in both directions. Both companies' vessels take motor vehicles, including rental cars and campervans, and all the ferries have a variety of onboard facilities, including viewing decks, television lounges, restaurants, cafes and private cabins for hire.

Details of the companies, the timetables and terminal locations can be seen at www.bluebridge.co.nz and interislander.co.nz.

SHIP COVE TODAY

Apart from a jetty and visitor facilities, the features of Ship Cove in outer Queen Charlotte Sound have changed little since Cook's visits there during the 1770s. The cove is a scenic reserve and is overlooked by forested hills and Mt Furneaux (823 metres), named after the commander of HMS *Adventure,* which moored in the cove in 1773. The shingle beach is sheltered from most winds. It is a short walk from the beach up to the stream from which the water barrels of Cook's ships were filled. There are picnic tables and public toilets on the cove's foreshore and leading up from the jetty is the first stage of the four-day Queen Charlotte Track.

Centrepiece on the foreshore is the Cook Monument, erected in 1913 and crowned with the anchor of a sailing ship. A series of interpretative panels, installed by the Department of Conservation and local iwi in 2006, provide details of the provenance of the site. They describe the pre-European history of the area, the five visits by Cook and his ships, and the interactions of his crews with local Maori.

Well worth the hike is a walk to the top of the hill above Ship Cove, on the first section of the track. It climbs up through native forest to a saddle, from where there are grand views of Resolution Bay and Endeavour Inlet, both named after Cook's ships.

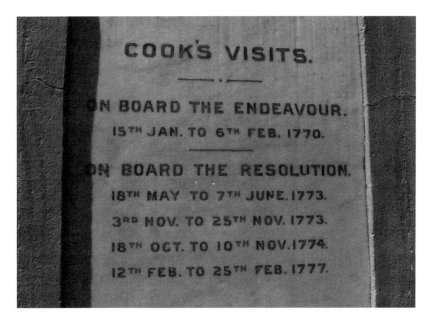

Plaque on the Cook Monument, Ship Cove

The Queen Charlotte Track

This 70-kilometre track, which can be walked or biked, spans almost the entire length of Queen Charlotte Sound and is one of the most popular in New Zealand. There are several accommodation options along the way: camp sites, guest houses and bed and breakfast establishments. The coastal and native bush scenery that can be viewed from the track is stunning.

The track begins at Ship Cove, then skirts Endeavour Inlet before crossing the Kenepuru Saddle. It then follows the spine of the long peninsula that borders the western side of Queen Charlotte Sound. In its final stages the track crosses the Te Mahia Saddle and bay before descending to Grove Arm and continuing along the coastline to Anakiwa.

Walking Distances and Times

Ship Cove to Endeavour Inlet: 15 kilometres, approx. 5–6 hours

Endeavour Inlet to Camp Bay: 11.5 kilometres, approx. 3.5–4 hours

Camp Bay to Torea Saddle: 23 kilometres, approx. 7–8 hours

Torea Saddle to Te Mahia Saddle: 8 kilometres, approx. 3–4 hours

Te Mahia Saddle to Anakiwa: 12.5 kilometres, approx. 3–4 hours

Biking Distances and Times

Ship Cove to Camp Bay: 26.5 kilometres, approx. 6 hours

Camp Bay to Torea Saddle: 23 kilometres, approx. 5 hours

Torea Saddle to Anakiwa: 20.5 kilometres, approx. 4 hours

NB: From Ship Cove to the Kenepuru Saddle the track is closed to mountain bikes from 1 December until 28 February.

THE SINKING OF THE *MIKHAIL LERMONTOV*

Port Gore is a broad bay in the Marlborough Sounds, between two headlands, Cape Lambert and Cape Jackson. Lying to the north-west of Ship Cove, Port Gore is named after Lieutenant John Gore, the American naval officer who sailed with Cook on his first and third world voyages.

Lying on her starboard side at the bottom of Port Gore is the wreck of a Soviet Union-era cruise ship, the *Mikhail Lermontov*. It has been there since the ship sank in 1986.

How on earth did a Soviet Union-era cruise ship end up on the bed of a bay in New Zealand's Marlborough Sounds?

Early on the morning of 16 February 1986 the *Mikhail Lermontov*, a 19,872-ton ocean liner owned by the Soviet Union's Baltic Shipping Company, was in Cook Strait, approaching the narrow entrance to Tory Channel. She had sailed out of Wellington Harbour the night before. In Wellington the ship had also taken aboard the pilot, Captain Don Jamison, the Picton harbourmaster. He was assisting the Russian master, Captain Vladislav Vorobyov.

The entrance to Tory Channel is narrow and bounded on both sides by high rock stacks, but the pass was deep and well-marked, and the *Mikhail Lermontov* passed through it without difficulty. The ship then entered much broader Tory Channel.

The *Mikhail Lermontov* spent the day moored alongside Picton's Waitohi wharf, allowing the mostly elderly Australian passengers time ashore and for selected visitors to come aboard. The ship was scheduled to sail again that afternoon, bound for Cape Jackson, Cape Farewell then the west coast of the South Island. On board were 372 passengers and 348 crew.

After her day in port, by the late afternoon the liner was sailing

133

out of Picton Harbour. Again in charge of the vessel was the pilot Don Jamison. Captain Vorobyov was below in his cabin resting, with another Russian officer on the bridge with Jamison.

By early evening the ship was sailing past Ship Cove, shadowing the western shoreline of Queen Charlotte Sound so that the passengers could get a closer view of the bay made famous from Cook's stopovers there. The cove was on the port (left) side of the ship.

After passing Ship Cove, Cannibal Cove and Waihi Point, the ship should have proceeded directly north, to cruise past Cape Jackson and on to Cape Farewell. But instead Jamison ordered the *Mikhail Lermontov* to go through the passage between Cape Jackson and Jackson Head.

The passage was too shallow. At 5.37pm, travelling at 15 knots, the ship struck Perham Rock, in the middle of the passage, about 5.5 metres below the waterline. Her hull was badly gashed on the port side below the waterline, and 30 metres aft of the bow thruster port.

The ship limped on into Port Gore, on the western side of Cape Jackson, with Captain Vorobyov endeavouring to beach her. But she was taking on too much water and at 8.30pm the passengers were ordered to abandon ship. With the aid of the crew and local rescue vessels all the passengers were transferred to several ships in the area, including the LPG tanker *Tarihiko* and the Cook Strait road-rail ferry *Arahura*.

As darkness descended on Port Gore the ship listed further to starboard, and twenty minutes after the last passenger was taken off she sank, four hours and twenty minutes after going aground. There was one casualty, 33-year-old crew engineer, Pavel Zagladimove, who went down with the ship. His remains were never found.

An enquiry into the sinking of the *Mikhail Lermontov* found that:

At the time of the grounding the ship's courses and speeds were being directed by Captain DI Jamison in the employ of the Marlborough Harbour Board as Harbourmaster and chief pilot. When Captain Jamison observed the passage between Cape Jackson and the Cape Jackson lighthouse...he made a sudden decision to navigate the ship through that passage. The decision to direct the ship through the channel was made by Captain Jamison without consulting any other person at the time...[1]

The then-New Zealand Minister of Transport, the Hon. Richard Prebble, later said of the captain's actions, 'Why he decided to guide the ship over a passage that he actually knew was too shallow, I don't think he'll ever be able to answer.'

An enquiry by the Soviet Government found that, 'the principal cause of the loss of the *Mikhail Lermontov* was the decision by the New Zealand pilot, Captain Don Jamison, to navigate the ship through the Cape Jackson Passage.'[2]

Captain Jamison himself was not charged with any offence and has never spoken in public about the loss of the ship. He subsequently took command of a livestock ferry operating between Picton and Wellington.

The Prime Minister of New Zealand at the time of the sinking was the Right Honourable David Lange. Not long before the sinking of the *Mikhail Lermontov* his government had declared the country to be nuclear-free, to the dismay of its military allies, notably the United States and Britain. When challenged by them over his government's nuclear-free policy, Lange quipped characteristically, 'Since World

War Two, New Zealand is the only country in the western world to have sunk a Russian ship.'

The wreck of the *Mikhail Lermontov* is a popular dive site, as it is one of the largest and most readily accessible shipwrecks in the world. The dive range varies from a 12-metre depth at the top of the wreck, to deep penetration and decompression dives to 36-metre depths. Care must be taken when diving the site and guides are strongly recommended. Three divers have died while exploring the wreck.

The wreck site is served by local dive shops in Picton. By road, Port Gore is reached by a long winding road out of Picton via Port Mahia, Portage and Kenepuru Head. One of the *Mikhail Lermontov*'s lifeboats sits outside a shopping mall in Picton.

The sinking of the *Mikhail Lermontov* invites this speculation: would James Cook have taken *Endeavour* or *Resolution* through the passage between Cape Jackson and Jackson Head? Possibly he would have, to save time. But he assuredly would also have had a man taking regular soundings with a lead-line ahead of his ship.

ENDEAVOUR'S VOYAGE: A MISSED RENDEZVOUS

When Cook's ship HMS *Resolution* first called at Ship Cove in May 1773, she was reunited with her consort vessel, HMS *Adventure*. The two vessels had become separated in the Antarctic Ocean three months earlier. In November 1773 the two ships became separated again, during a gale off the south-east coast of the North Island. Furneaux and *Adventure* first took shelter at Uawa-Tolaga Bay, and eventually made it back to Ship Cove, on 30 November 1773. There they found a message in a bottle, left by

Cook, buried at the foot of a tree, stating that he and *Resolution* were departing to explore the 'Southern parts of the Pacific Ocean.' The date was 25 November 1773. The two ships had missed one another by just five days.

Furneaux and his men, no doubt deeply disappointed at missing the rendezvous with Cook, prepared for their own departure from Ship Cove. *Adventure* had to be repaired after her battering from the gales, and fully provisioned.

On 17 December Furneaux despatched a midshipman, John Rowe, and nine others, in the ship's cutter to a bay Cook had named Grass Cove, on the other side of Queen Charlotte Sound. Rowe and the others were to cut fresh greens as part of the provisioning for *Adventure*'s impending voyage.

The cutter failed to return to Ship Cove that day. The next day Furneaux sent Lieutenant James Burney with a boat crew and ten marines, to search for the missing party.

At East Bay, on Arapawa Island, Burney's men had their suspicions aroused when they saw some Maori behaving aggressively on shore. Firing guns to alert the missing men of their presence, Furneaux's boat turned into the channel separating Pickersgill Island from the shore. At East Bay they saw a large canoe guarded by two men. After the guards ran into the bush Burney inspected the canoe and in it found some shoes belonging to one of the missing men. Nearby they also found several food baskets containing roasted human flesh. One of the body parts was the hand of Thomas Hill, identified because it bore the tattooed initials 'TH'. Hill had acquired the tattoo in Tahiti.

Burney's party saw smoke coming from around the point, at Grass Cove. After rowing into the bay they found more canoes pulled up on the shore and a crowd of people gathered there. When these Maori taunted and threatened Burney and his men, he ordered the marines to fire into the crowd. After two volleys of musket fire the Maori ran up into the forest. Then, moving up onto the foreshore, Burney and his men came upon 'such a shocking scene of Carnage & Barbarity as can never be mentioned or thought of, but with horror.'[3]

The dismembered remains of Rowe and the nine other men were scattered about the ground and dogs were chewing on their entrails. 'The sailors' hearts and heads had been cut from their bodies and eaten in the *whangai hau* ceremony, destroying the mana of the victims and leaving their kinsfolk bereft of ancestral protection.'[4]

Fearing they would be attacked themselves, Burney and the others hastily gathered up the body parts, damaged the Maori canoes, and rowed back across the sound to Ship Cove and Adventure. The remains of the massacred men were later committed to the sea.

On 23 December 1773 *Adventure* unmoored and set sail for the eastern Pacific. This time Furneaux's ship was not reunited with Cook's *Resolution*. Instead Furneaux took *Adventure* around Cape Horn and eventually back to England via Cape Town. This vessel thus became the first to ever circumnavigate the globe from west to east.

Until the gruesome discovery at Grass Cove, Lieutenant James Burney had kept a colourful journal of his voyage on *Adventure*. But so shocked was the young officer by the discovery of the massacre that his journal entries ceased forthwith.

When Cook returned to Queen Charlotte Sound on his last voyage, in February 1777, he was urged by his men to take revenge on the Maori responsible for the Grass Cove killings. A chief called Kahura was known to have led the massacre. But to the anger and mystification of his men, Cook took no retaliation against Kahura. Instead he welcomed the chief aboard *Resolution* and encouraged Johann Webber to draw his portrait. This was a deeply unpopular gesture with both Cook's men and the local Maori, who didn't like Kahura either.

Today Grass Cove is known as Wharehunga Bay. A recreational reserve on the west coast of Arapawa Island, the bay is now as peaceful a place as can be imagined.

HMS *RESOLUTION*

For his second world voyage (1772–1775), the principal aim of which was to discover if a Great Unknown Southern Continent existed somewhere in the Southern Hemisphere, James Cook insisted that two ships be taken. This was a precautionary measure, since he had come close to losing *Endeavour* and her crew when she went aground on the Great Barrier Reef in May, 1770. Taking just one vessel was too risky.

The two ships purchased by the Navy Board for Cook's second world voyage were both former colliers, built by Fishburn's at Whitby. They were called originally the *Marquis of Granby* and *Marquis of Rockingham,* then were renamed *Drake* and *Raleigh*. Later they were renamed again as HMS *Resolution* and HMS *Adventure,* to avoid the names of the two English buccaneers giving offence to the Spanish authorities.

Fitted out at the Deptford naval dock and classed as a sloop, HMS *Resolution* (469 tonnes) became Cook's favourite ship. Intending to sail again with Cook as naturalist, Joseph Banks had expensive additions and modifications made to *Resolution.* He insisted that her waist be raised and a whole new deck added, to accommodate an inflated entourage that he insisted accompany him.

After these additions were made, a sea trial showed immediately that they made the vessel top-heavy and hence unsafe. Cook then insisted that the additions be demolished. Their removal infuriated Banks, who promptly withdrew from the expedition. He was replaced as naturalist by a Prussian, Reinhold Forster, and his seventeen-year-old son, George. *Resolution*'s escort vessel, HMS *Adventure* (341 tonnes), was commanded by Tobias Furneaux.

Resolution was the first ship to ever cross both the Antarctic and the Arctic Circles, since Cook again chose to use her on his third world voyage (1776–1780). However *Resolution* was not well prepared for the extreme conditions this arduous expedition involved. The Navy Board had given more priority to maintaining the nation's fleet involved in defending England's colonies in North America against the insurgency there. Consequently, Cook found to his chagrin that *Resolution*'s decks now leaked and her rigging was in poor condition. Her consort vessel, HMS *Discovery,* was also in a substandard state. This caused Cook great concern throughout the third world voyage.

HMS *Resolution* later served as a transport vessel, then as a whaler in Arctic waters. She sank at her moorings in 1793, in

Newport Harbour, near where her Cook voyaging predecessor, HMS *Endeavour* lay on the harbour floor.

MV *Pembroke* at Supper Cove, Dusky Sound

CHAPTER SEVEN

DUSKY SOUND

*Soon after my return to the Ship Mr Pickersgill returned also
and reported that he had also succeeded in finding a good harbour with
every other conveniency.*

Dusky Sound is a deep fiord in the coast of Fiordland, in the extreme south-west of the South Island. Created by glaciers during the last Ice Age, these rivers of ice flowed down from the alpine interior and reamed out deep troughs in the landscape. After the Ice Age ended, about 12,000 years ago, the troughs were invaded by the sea. As a consequence the coast of this part of New Zealand is heavily indented with sounds whose walls are high, precipitous and densely forested. Fiordland has the highest rainfall in New Zealand, averaging 8000 millimetres annually, so another feature of the sounds is the many waterfalls that cascade down their sides.

Dusky Sound is 45 kilometres long and eight kilometres wide at its Tasman Sea entrance. Within the sound are many islands, large and small, walled in by ramparts of rock hundreds of metres high. The largest of these—named by Cook 'Resolution Island'—is 208 square kilometres. It lies to the north of the sound's entrance. Within the sound, Long Island and Cooper Island are also substantial. The mountainous terrain and dense forests surrounding Dusky Sound, and its isolation in the extreme south-west of the South Island, make it one of the least accessible parts of New Zealand. It is separated from the rest of the country by the Southern Alps, the South Island's backbone, created by the meeting of two great tectonic plates, the Pacific Plate and the Australian Plate.

Dusky Sound is part of Fiordland National Park, the largest such park in the country and part of the South-West New Zealand World Heritage area.

There are no roads to Dusky Sound, just one walking track, the toughest in New Zealand. Otherwise, those who wish to visit the sound must gain access to it by helicopter, charter vessel or private boat. The charter launch MV *Milford Wanderer* takes passengers on scheduled cruises of the sound and the MV *Pembroke** offers a boutique experience for groups of up to eight passengers, for sightseeing, fishing, diving or hunting.

Dusky Sound is largely unchanged from the pristine condition it was in during Cook's stay. There are few facilities anywhere in the sound apart from a cray fisherman's pontoon and a few pipes that vessels can use to fill their water tanks. There are also some DOC huts for conservation workers and a trampers' hut near the end of the Dusky Track, at the head of the sound.

The rest is unchanged, pristine wilderness and geographic splendour. Waterfalls pour down the sound's precipitous walls, forests reach the water's edge, gauzy mists swirl about the tops and rain showers sweep in regularly from the west. Such is the volume of rainfall that Dusky, like Fiordland's other sounds, has a fresh water lens up to five metres in depth, that floats on the surface and which is stained brown, like tea without milk. This colour is derived from tannins in the bark of the southern beech trees that clothe the surrounding land.

Dusky is home to a variety of fauna. Fur seals bask on its rocky islets and coasts, pods of dolphins cavort in its waters and mollymawks (a species of albatross) feed on its fish.

During their breeding season the distinctive Fiordland crested penguins (in Maori, tawaki) frequent the sound. Anchor Island, just inside the entrance, is a bird sanctuary, home to many endangered species of native birds, including the kakapo, a flightless, nocturnal, ground-dwelling parrot. Anchor Island is also the place where the first European-style house and the first European-type boat were built in New Zealand.

As the light constantly changes so too do the moods of Dusky Sound. Sunlight illuminates the forest canopy and is reflected from the water. Sunsets gild the sound's surface and highlight the mountain tops. The snow-covered alpine backdrop, away to the east, glows in the setting sun.

Grandeur is too feeble an adjective for Dusky Sound.

The fishing here is excellent. New Zealand's finest eating fish, blue cod, can be taken readily on a line, while crayfish can easily be caught using a snorkel or in baited pots. Seven Gill sharks abound, and while they are not preferred eating, are good bait for line fishing or the crayfish pots.

A modern chart of Dusky Sound reveals the enduring relationship between the sound and James Cook's 1773 sojourn there, nearly two-and-a-half centuries ago. Many of the landmarks were named during HMS *Resolution*'s six-week visit. The most prominent of these are Cooper Island, Long Island, Resolution Island and Five Fingers Peninsula.

Some places were named after incidents that occurred during Cook's stay. The most significant of these is Astronomer's Point, a short walk up through the forest from a mooring in Pickersgill Harbour, named after Richard Pickersgill, third lieutenant on *Resolution*. It was Pickersgill who discovered the sheltered inlet where Resolution was moored.

Astronomer's Point is a fifteen-metre-high hill where Cook and his astronomer William Wales took their astronomical observations during the visit. *Resolution* was made fast to a handy overhanging tree branch and a party of men was sent to the top of the hillock to make a clearing in the virgin forest. This was done so that Cook and his astronomer could make unimpeded observations and thus accurately establish the point's coordinates.

After taking observations of the sun, moon and stars from the clearing, Wales calculated the position of Astronomer's Point to be longitude 166° 18' 9" East, and latitude 45° 47' 26" South. These coordinates were only slightly inaccurate. A calculation with modern instruments gives the coordinates of the point as longitude 166° 33' 56" East and latitude 45° 47' 45" South.

Today a boardwalk and steps lead up to a viewing platform near the top of the hill. On the hill itself, amid the forest and covered with moss and ferns, are the stumps of some of the trees felled by Cook's men. An information panel beside the boardwalk explains the historical significance of Astronomer's Point.

Inland from the hill a hiking trail follows the course of a stream, which flows into the inlet where *Resolution* was moored. Lake Forster is a half-hour walk away. A glacial lake surrounded by dense forest, it was named after the father and son naturalists aboard *Resolution*, Johann and George Forster.

Branches of Dusky Sound such as Supper Cove, Luncheon Cove, Duck Cove and Wet Jacket Arm were also named by Cook after events that occurred during *Resolution*'s visit.

Luncheon Cove is on Anchor Island, three miles from Pickersgill Harbour, near the entrance to the sound. A secluded inlet, Luncheon Cove's rocky shore is home to a fur seal colony. From the late-eighteenth century onwards the seals were hunted ruthlessly for their skins. A promontory within Luncheon Cove was the site of the first European house built in New Zealand, in 1792. It housed some of the sealers who had come to slaughter the creatures in their thousands. Today the fur seals are a protected species.

From the head of Luncheon Cove a track leads up through the forest, following a stream bed. The going is made difficult by the twisted roots of forest giants, mainly the podocarps rimu, miro and totara, but the forest is primeval and resonates with the calls of bellbirds, tui and pigeons. The track leads to Lake Kirirua, which is enclosed by the forest. Although the climb is testing, the view of the lake upon arrival makes it well worth the effort.

*HMV *Pembroke* was the name of a naval vessel on which James Cook served, first in the Bay of Biscay, then off the east coast of North America, from1757–1759. MV *Pembroke* of Dusky Sound is named after her.

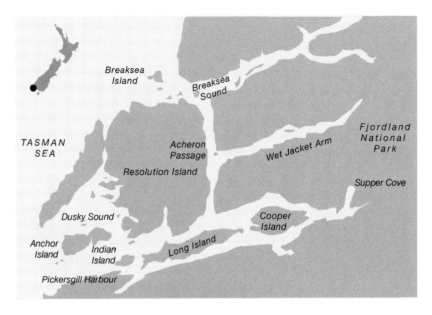

Map of Dusky Sound

RESOLUTION'S VOYAGE: JAMES COOK & DUSKY SOUND

On 14 March 1770, while on his circumnavigation of the South Island in HMS *Endeavour*, James Cook saw in the distance the entrance to Dusky Sound. But he sailed on past it, incurring the ire of naturalist Joseph Banks, who was impatient to go ashore and 'botanise' around the sound because *Endeavour* had not touched land since leaving Ship Cove in Queen Charlotte Sound, five weeks earlier. However Cook did not wish to enter what he named 'Dusky Bay'—because of the darkness of the coast—fearing that once within it *Endeavour* might become embayed because of the prevailing south-westerly winds.

148

Accordingly, Cook sailed past the sound and maintained a northward course along the South Island's west coast.

It was a very different story three years later. In March 1773 Cook and HMS *Resolution* had been weeks in the waters of the Antarctic Ocean, tacking among icebergs and battered by gales and snow storms. After more than '117 days at sea in which time we have Sailed 36,660 Leagues [11,000 nautical miles] without once having sight of land,'[1] Cook's men and his ship were badly in need of recuperation. Hence his decision to take the ship to an anchorage in the nearest favourable environment. He had not forgotten glimpsing the entrance to 'Dusky Bay' three years earlier.

On 26 March 1773, Cook recorded:

> *...we steered and entred Dusky Bay about Noon in the mouth of which we found 44 fathom water, a Sandy Bottom. Here we found a vast swell roll in from the sw...we were however too far advanced to return and therefore pushed on not doubting but what we should find anchorage, for in this Bay we were all strangers...*[2]

After he succeeded in sailing into the vast inlet and discovered its true nature, Cook amended the name to 'Dusky Sound'.

Cook's men were delighted with the sound. For example *Resolution*'s young naturalist George Forster wrote in his journal:

> *The weather was delightfully fair, and genially warm, when compared with what we had lately experienced; and we glided along*

by insensible degrees, wafted by light airs, past numerous rocky islands, each of which was covered with wood and shrubberies, where numerous evergreens were sweetly contrasted and mingled with the various shades of autumnal yellow. Flocks of aquatic birds enlivened the rocky shores, and the whole country resounded with the wild notes of the feathered tribe.[3]

Not long after their arrival, *Resolution*'s third lieutenant, Richard Pickersgill, came upon a suitable mooring at the head of a snug bay with five fathoms of water. The ship was hauled stern first into the cove and moored to the trees. There was a clear stream nearby and a fallen tree extending over the cove provided convenient access from ship to shore.

George Forster also described their mooring:

At nine o'clock we got under sail and went into Pickersgill Harbour, one of those examined the previous day, where the ship was moored head and stern in a small creek, and so near the shore, that we could reach it by means of a stage of a few planks. Nature had assisted us for this purpose with a large tree, projecting in a horizontal position over the water...[4]

After the gruelling weeks in the Antarctic Ocean the men of *Resolution* fell upon the provender of Dusky Sound like famished men at a banquet. The place was a rich source of fresh food and water. There were ducks in abundance and fish were plentiful: blue cod, tarakihi, crayfish and groper, with small sharks either eaten or used for bait. Mollymawks, a handsome seabird belonging to the albatross family, were also shot and eaten. Fat fur seals were abundant and since they lived in crowded colonies, made easy targets.

Their carcasses made good steaks, their fat was rendered into lamp-oil, their skins were used to protect the ship's chafed backstays and lifts.[5]

There were other valuable resources. The tall straight rimu, totara and miro trees which grew around the sound were ideal for the ship's carpenters to fashion into replacement spars for *Resolution*. Trunks of manuka cut into suitable lengths made ideal fuel for the galley's firebox.

The Swedish naturalist Anders Sparrman, who had joined *Resolution* in Cape Town, was another of the ship's company who relished the environment of Dusky Sound. He wrote:

Enormous mast-trees raised their cedar-like tops proudly and majestically high above the other tall trees in the valleys; the flight of sea birds and pelicans along the shores, and various chirpings and pleasant songs of the land-birds in the nearby dells, enlivened the whole scene. What a heavenly contrast to storms, ice, and the occasional scream of a penguin in a boundless Antarctic sea![6]

The sound was sheltered from almost all winds, and the frequent heavy rainfall kept water cascading down its almost-vertical slopes. *Resolution*'s butts were filled from one of these waterfalls.

Resolution was in Dusky Sound from 27 March until early May. During this time Cook probed and surveyed the sound and produced a detailed chart of its islands, inlets and waterways. He named many of its geographic features, including: Astronomer's Point, Anchor Island, Woodhen Cove, Shag Islands, Duck Cove, Seal Isles, Goose Cove, Wet Jacket Arm, Cascade Cove, Long Island, Indian Island, Luncheon Cove, Supper Cove and Shark Cove.

There were only a few Maori living in Dusky Sound at this time, but Cook made contact with an extended family living on one of its islands, members of the Ngati Mamoe iwi. These were evidently a migratory group, visiting the sound they called 'Tamatea' to hunt and gather food, especially seals.

Gifts were exchanged with the family, and later other Maori visited *Resolution*. The ship's official artist was William Hodges, whose brief from the Admiralty was, 'To give a more perfect idea than can be formed by written description.' In Dusky Sound Hodges painted a portrait of the Maori whanau, entitling it, *Family in Dusky Bay, New Zealand*. Today in the sound it's possible to see the very point on 'Indian Island' upon which the family stand in the Hodges portrait. Later the artist also produced an oil painting entitled *Waterfall in Dusky Bay, New Zealand* and portrayed the north entrance to Dusky Bay and Breaksea Island.*

Naturalist illustrator George Forster produced exquisite drawings of the birds, fish and plants of Dusky Sound. These included a kokopu, the native trout, the New Zealand falcon and the grey duck.

By early May *Resolution* was fully provisioned and her crew refreshed. The carpenters and sail-makers had made the necessary repairs and the ship carried ample supplies of smoked fish, freshly-brewed rimu-manuka beer and enough fresh duck and seal meat for the next leg of the voyage. Dusky Sound had indeed been bounteous to the Resolutions.

The ship was unmoored from Pickersgill Harbour on 11 May. Rather than work the ship back to the entrance by which they had entered, *Resolution* made egress from Dusky Sound via a different pass. This was a long, narrow, north–south passage that had been discovered by the ship's sailing master, Joseph Gilbert. This provided a more direct outlet to the open sea. Today called Acheron Passage, the corridor was bounded by massive Resolution Island to the west before it opened out to another sound which Cook named 'Break Sea'.

In open water once again, *Resolution* stood to the northward, bound for Ship Cove in Queen Charlotte Sound. There, after surviving a water spout in Cook's Strait, the ship kept a designated rendezvous with its consort vessel, HMS *Adventure*, from whom *Resolution* had become separated in the dense fog of the Antarctic Ocean, three months earlier.

*Hodges later also produced a painting he entitled *A View of Cape Stephens in Cook's Straits with Waterspout*. It shows the *Resolution* between Dusky Sound and Queen Charlotte Sound, in May 1773, when a waterspout struck. This powerful painting emphasises the vulnerability of Cook's ship in the face of extreme elements, an incident which was one of the most frightening of his second world voyage. The painting, along with other of Hodges' works, is held in the National Maritime Museum, Greenwich, London.

THE DUSKY TRACK

The Dusky Track in Fiordland National Park is 84-kilometres long and takes up to ten days to walk. Because of the ruggedness of the terrain it crosses, high levels of fitness are required for the traverse.

Trampers can start the walk either at Lake Manapouri or Lake Hauroko. The latter is New Zealand's deepest known lake and comprises a dramatic introduction to the Dusky Track. There is a regular boat service across Lake Manapouri, but a crossing of Lake Hauroko must be arranged before commencing the walk. Float Plane or helicopter access can be arranged to Supper Cove, at the head of Dusky Sound.

The Dusky Track crosses two alpine passes and rises to a maximum height of 1100 metres. It is prone to flooding after heavy rain and contains mud pits, many tree roots and some very steep sections. There are fifteen three-wire bridges. Thus it is suitable only for very fit, experienced and well-equipped trampers. It cannot be guided and there is no camping possible along the way.

There are eight huts on the track. A portable stove and fuel must be carried by trampers as dry firewood is scarce at the hut sites. No booking is necessary, but hut tickets are required. These can be purchased from the Department of Conservation, Lakefront Drive, Te Anau. Phone: 03 249 7924.

Email: fiordlandvc@doc.govt.nz.

Website: www.fiordlandnz.com.

The stages of the track are as follows:

- ॐ Lake Hauroko to Halfway Hut, 5–6 hours
- ॐ Halfway Hut to Lake Roe, 5 hours
- ॐ Lake Roe to Loch Maree, 4–5 hours.

From Loch Maree Hut a spur track branches to the west, along the Seaforth River, which is subject to flooding. This spur leads to the Supper Cove Hut, near the head of Dusky Sound. The hut is on a small terrace, just south of Hilda Burn, and has twelve bunks. Supper Cove provides good fishing, so taking a line is recommended. A dinghy stored in a shed below the hut is available for public use, but extreme care must be taken on the sound's waters, as weather conditions can change very quickly.

After returning to Loch Maree, the Dusky Track continues north in these stages:

- ॐ Loch Maree to Kintail, 4–5 hours
- ॐ Kintail–Centre Pass–Upper Spey, 5–6 hours
- ॐ Upper Spey–Track Head, 4–5 hours
- ॐ Track Head to West Arm, Lake Manapouri, 45 minutes

Sounds' discovery expeditions

A five-day/four-night cruise can be taken on Dusky and Breaksea Sounds, allowing passengers to gain access to these remote fiords. The purpose-built MV *Milford Wanderer* cruises in the wake of James Cook's visit to these sounds in 1773. The cruise includes one-way or return heli-transfers. Specialist nature guides on the vessel provide commentaries on the sounds and give talks in the evening. There are also guided walks through the forests and along the shorelines. The vessel's tender craft and kayaks allow close exploration of the sounds' coves and shorelines.

Phone: 03 249 6000; Freephone within New Zealand 0800 656501. Email: contact@realjourneys.co.nz.

Website: www.discoveryexpeditions.co.nz.

It's also possible to take day or overnight cruises on Fiordland's Doubtful Sound, to the north of Dusky. Doubtful is an equally spectacular fiord, also named by Cook, this time in 1770 on HMS *Endeavour*. The ship sailed past the entrance to the sound and Cook named it 'Doubtful' because of his uncertainty as to whether, if he entered it, he could subsequently sail out of it.

As is the case with Dusky Sound, there is no direct road access to Doubtful Sound. Getting there requires a road connection on SH 6 from Queenstown to Manapouri or on SH 95 from Te Anau to Manapouri. A cruise is then required across Lake Manapouri, followed by a coach trip over Wilmot Pass to the head of Doubtful Sound, where the cruise vessel is boarded.

Phone: Freephone within NZ: 0800 65 65 01. Websites: www.realjourneys.co.nz; www.fiordlandcharters.co.nz.

For helicopter services into Dusky and Doubtful Sounds: Email info@southernlakeshelicopters.co.nz.

Website: www.teanauhelicopters.com.

THE FIRST BEER BREWED IN NEW ZEALAND

Lieutenant Charles Clerke, who sailed with Cook on all three world voyages, was a keen amateur brewer. On the 1772–1775 voyage he was second lieutenant on

HMS *Resolution*, and began brewing beer in the Atlantic, on the way to Cape Town. He noted in his journal, rather defensively:

11 puncheons [barrels] which proved a salutary and I think pleasant drink. Many of the people disliked it vastly –preferred water to it— but I believe it was more caprice than any absolute distaste for it. I've seen many whims of this kind among seaman…put the remains which was nine casks down in the hold after having brewed.[7]

It was in Dusky Sound that the onboard brewing of beer really came into its own. After *Resolution*'s arrival in the sound the sloop was moored in a branch of what Cook named 'Pickersgill Harbour'. A clear stream flowed into the cove and thick forest grew all around it. The vegetation included the large coniferous rimu tree and manuka shrubs, also known as 'tea tree'. Some of the crew began brewing beer, using this vegetation as a base. After noting the process, Cook wrote:

We first made a strong decoction of the leaves or small branches of the Spruce [rimu] tree & Tea shrub [manuka] by boiling them three or four hours, or untill the bark will strip with ease from the branches, then take the leaves or branches out of the Copper and mix with the liquor the proper quantity of Melasses and Inspissated [a process of thickening by dehydration] Juce, one Gallon of the former and three of the latter is sufficient to make a puncheon or 80 gallons of Beer, let this mixture just boil and then put it into the Cask and to it add an equal quantity of Cold Water more or less according to your taste and the strength of the decoction, when the whole is but milk warm put in a little grounds of Beer or yeast, if you have any, or any thing else that will cause fermentation and in a few days the Beer will be fit to drink.[8]

If just the rimu leaves were used, the resulting beer was too harsh, but if manuka foliage was added, Cook wrote, 'the Beer was exceedingly Palatable and esteemed by every one on board.'

Naturalist Sparrman declared of the Dusky Sound brew, 'After a small amount of rum or arrack has been added, with some brown sugar, and stirred into this really pleasant, refreshing, and healthy drink, it bubbled and tasted rather like champagne.'

The beer also possessed slight anti-scorbutic (scurvy-combating) qualities, which boosted the crew's health, along with their general well-being. Beer brewed from the leaves of the rimu tree and the manuka shrub was later also made when *Resolution* and *Adventure* were moored at Ship Cove, in Queen Charlotte Sound.

Since the beginning of the twenty-first century there has been a proliferation of boutique brewing throughout New Zealand, in the main centres and in regions such as Motueka in the South Island, the country's main hop-growing province. By 2016 there were over 100 craft breweries operating in New Zealand, and exports of their beers were growing, especially to Singapore and China.

One of these brews, Wigram Captain Cook Spruce Beer, is based on James Cook's original Dusky Sound recipe, being flavoured with 'spruce' and 'tea tree' leaves. The label of this beer features the Nathaniel Dance portrait of Captain Cook.

Another beer inspired by the 1773 brewing is 'Captain Cooker' manuka beer. Named after the hogs descended from the English varieties released in New Zealand by Cook, this beer is commonly referred to as 'The Pig'. The product is promoted by a well-known country pub, the Mussel Inn, which is in rural Motueka and is notable for its food and live music. Captain Cooker is a red-brown, all-malt beer flavoured with the tips of the manuka bush and organically grown organic hops. This beer is also brewed in Belgium, Utah and the United Kingdom.

THE NEW ZEALAND FUR SEAL—*ARCTOCEPHALUS FORSTERI*

Cook and his men found the fur seals of Dusky Sound a readily available source of food. Pre-European Maori knew this, too, and hunted the seals for food and their skins. After the arrival of Europeans in the late eighteenth and early nineteenth centuries, the seals were plundered for their skins. A gang left on the shore of Dusky Sound in 1792 was collected the following year along with 4500 skins. This wholesale slaughter took the seals to the edge of extinction.

Since then the seal population has recovered and today totals about 100,000 animals. They are found on rocky shores around the three main islands of the country, as well as the Chatham Islands and the sub-Antarctic Islands. Known as kekeno to Maori, they feed mainly on squid and small fish and can dive deeper and longer than any other seal, as deep as 238 metres and for up to eleven minutes. They feed mostly at night, when their prey is closer to the surface.

The pointy-nosed seal has long, pale whiskers and its body is covered with two layers of fur. Their pelt is dark brown on the back and lighter below, and when wet looks almost black. The mature females are a maximum of 1.5 metres long and weigh 30–50 kilograms. Adult males have a maximum length of 2.5 metres and weigh 90–150 kilograms.

Every year the seals return to the same area for the breeding season, which occurs from mid-November to mid-January. These rookeries are known as 'haul-outs'. Here dominant bulls put on displays of glaring, posturing and fighting with other males just before the breeding season, to gain territory. A male may mate with many females in a single breeding season; a female will have her first pup between four and six years of age, and will continue to give birth to a single pup every year until her death.

Pups are suckled for about 300 days. The females alternate foraging trips for periods of up to twenty days at sea to feed, with attendance periods at the rookery to suckle the pup. As the year progresses and the pups grow stronger, the females take longer and longer foraging trips. Fur seals live on average from fourteen to seventeen years.

In 1978 fur seals were fully covered by the *Marine Mammals Protection Act,* and they have continued to grow in numbers ever since. Total numbers increased by 25 percent per year between 1982 and 1994, research in Otago showed. Human activities are the main threat to the seals; they can be captured and accidentally drowned during trawling and long line fishing operations. Great white sharks are their main natural predators.

Occasionally fur seals come ashore in unexpected places, such as coastal paddocks, suburban streets and creeks. They have been known to enter houses if a door has been left open. One seal even entered and made itself at home in a suburban car-wash in Auckland city.

Although fur seals are lovely looking creatures, they are feral and should be treated respectfully. Always watch them from a distance, do not attempt to get close to them.

ENDEAVOUR'S VOYAGE: THE DEPARTURE

From *James Cook's Journal*, Sunday, 1 April 1770:

I have before made mention of our quiting New-Zeland with an intention to steer to the westward which we accordingly did take our departure from Cape Fare-well in the Latitude of 40° 30' and Longitude 185° 58' w from Greenwich, which bore from us at 5pm West 18° north distance 12 Miles. After this we steer'd NW and WNW in order to give it a good birth until 8 oClock am at which time we steer'd West having the advantage of a fresh gale at NBE.[9]

Thus was described James Cook's first departure from New Zealand, whose islands he had charted meticulously over the preceding six months. *Endeavour* was now bound for New Holland-Australia, whose east coast Cook would also survey thoroughly.

Cook must have looked back with satisfaction at what he had achieved during his circumnavigation of the long land of New Zealand. He had surveyed its coasts, he had given names to many of its geographic features, he had made meaningful contact with its indigenous people and had claimed the new land and its many islands for his sovereign, George III. From now on, in Cook's mind, New Zealand would be forever British.

But Cook was far from finished with New Zealand. He would return in 1773 (on two occasions), in 1774, and finally, in 1777. However, the principal charting had been accomplished on his first voyage. On the later visits he would use the country's anchorages—mainly Ship Cove in Queen Charlotte Sound—as places to provision his other voyaging ships, HMS *Resolution,* HMS *Adventure* and HMS *Discovery.*

For these reasons, the names 'New Zealand' and 'James Cook' will be always connected.

APPENDICES

BIBLIOGRAPHY AND SOURCES

INTRODUCTION

1. Michael King, *The Penguin History of New Zealand*, page 91.

2. JC Beaglehole (ed.), *The Voyage of the* Endeavour *1768–1771*, page 168.

3. Michael King, *The Penguin History of New Zealand*, page 108.

CHAPTER ONE

1. JC Beaglehole (ed.), *The Voyage of the* Endeavour *1768–1771*, page 168.

2. Sir Joseph Banks, *The* Endeavour *Journal of Joseph Banks*, online at Project Gutenberg Australia.

CHAPTER THREE

1. JC Beaglehole (ed.), *The Voyage of the* Endeavour *1768–1771*, page 194–195.

2. Kerry Howe, *To the Islands*, page 31.

3. Anne Salmond, *Two Worlds*, page 87.

4. Anne Salmond, *The Trial of the Cannibal Dog: Captain Cook in the South Seas*, page 130.

5. Michael King, *The Penguin History of New Zealand*, page 108.

6. JC Beaglehole (ed.), *The Voyage of the* Endeavour *1768–1771*, page 197.

7. Sir Joseph Banks, *The* Endeavour *Journal of Joseph Banks*, online at Project Gutenberg Australia.

8. Sir Joseph Banks, *The* Endeavour *Journal of Joseph Banks,* online at Project Gutenberg Australia.

CHAPTER FOUR

1. JC Beaglehole (ed.), *The Voyage of the* Endeavour *1768–1771,* page 210.

2. Sir Joseph Banks, *The* Endeavour *Journal of Joseph Banks,* online at Project Gutenberg Australia.

3. A Charles Begg and Neil C Begg, *James Cook in New Zealand,* page 47.

4. Sir Joseph Banks, *The* Endeavour *Journal of Joseph Banks,* online at Project Gutenberg Australia.

CHAPTER FIVE

1. JC Beaglehole (ed.), *The Voyage of the* Endeavour *1768–1771,* page 230.

2. JC Beaglehole (ed.), *The Voyage of the* Endeavour *1768–1771,* page 232.

CHAPTER SIX

1. Tom O'Connor, *Death of a Cruise Ship,* Cape Catley, 1999, page 151.

2. Tom O'Connor, *Death of a Cruise Ship,* page 195.

3. Anne Salmond, *The Trial of the Cannibal Dog: Captain Cook in the South Seas,* page 229.

4. Anne Salmond, *The Trial of the Cannibal Dog: Captain Cook in the South Seas,* pages 3–4.

CHAPTER SEVEN

1. Rob Rundle, *Cook: From Sailor to Legend,* page 313.

2. JC Beaglehole (ed.), *The Voyage of* Resolution *and* Adventure *1772–1775,* page 109.

3. George Forster, *A Voyage Round the World in His Majesty's Sloop Resolution, commanded by Capt. James Cook during the Years 1772, 3, 4, 5,* from Chapter V. Forster's account is online at: pacific. obdurodon.org/ForsterGeorgeComplete.html

George Forster was an immensely talented young man. Upon his return to England the naturalist and illustrator published an account of his voyage with Cook. Called *A Voyage Round the World* (1777). The book contains a wealth of scientific information collected by Forster during Cook's second voyage. The publication was a critical and commercial success. In recognition of his multiple talents, George was made a member of the Royal Society in the year of his book's publication, at the age of just 22. An edition of his *A Voyage Round the World* was published by the University of Hawaii Press in 2000.

4. As above.

5. Allan Villiers, *Captain Cook The Seamen's Seaman,* 1967, page 171.

6. Richard Hough, *Captain James Cook: A Biography,* page 209.

7. Richard Hough, *Captain James Cook: A Biography,* page 200.

8. JC Beaglehole (ed.), *The Voyage of* Resolution *and* Adventure *1772–1775,* Part II, page 137.

9. JC Beaglehole (ed.), *The Voyage of the* Endeavour *1768–1771,* page 294–295.

FURTHER READING

The volume of published material on the life and achievements of James Cook is immense. A guide book such as this one is necessarily a summation of Cook's visits to New Zealand. For those wishing to fill in the gaps in Cook's story, or to gain a larger picture of his life and achievements, the following works are recommended.

Cook: From Sailor to Legend by Rob Mundle (HarperCollins, 2013). A specialist maritime journalist, broadcaster and blue water sailor, Mundle writes of Cook's achievements with the inside knowledge of another man of the sea.

Captain James Cook: A Biography by Richard Hough (Hodder & Stoughton, 1994). A former Royal Navy man himself, Hough writes engagingly of Cook's life from a thoroughly English point of view.

James Cook and New Zealand by A Charles Begg and Neil C Begg (AR Shearer, Government Printer, Wellington, 1969). Produced for the bicentenary of Cook's first visit to New Zealand, this is a detailed study of the places the navigator called at, and the events which occurred during his visits.

Resolution by the prolific English novelist AN Wilson (Atlantic Books, London, 2016) is a fictionalised account of the short but eventful life of George Forster (1754–98), who sailed with his father Johann on Cook's *Resolution*. Aged only seventeen when the ship sailed, George proved to be a skilled illustrator, a dedicated naturalist and a popular crew member, unlike his father, who was a tiresome and peevish shipmate. Wilson's novel covers the voyage and the post-voyage events in George's life, particularly his political activism, which ended with his death in Paris during the French revolution.

Sailing with Cook: Inside the Private Journal of James Burney RN by Suzanne Rickard (National Library of Australia, 2015). A personal account of Cook's second voyage, written for Burney's family and friends. He closely observed and recorded native cultures, until the massacre at Ship Cove in 1777 traumatised him. Thereafter he wrote no more.

The Life of Captain James Cook by JC Beaglehole (Stanford University Press, 1974). A scholarly biography by the acknowledged authority on the navigator and his achievements. Beaglehole's other monumental works are those that cover the voyage of *Endeavour* and Cook's and Joseph Banks's journals from that voyage. These are: *The Journals of Captain James Cook on His Voyages of Discovery, Volume 1 The Voyages of the* Endeavour *1768–1771* (Cambridge University Press, Hakluyt Society, 1955) and *The Endeavour Journal of Joseph Banks 1768–1771* (Angus & Robertson, 1963), both edited by JC Beaglehole. *The* Endeavour *Journal of Joseph Banks* is also available online at Project Gutenberg Australia.

The Trial of the Cannibal Dog: Captain Cook in the South Seas by Anne Salmond (Penguin Books, 2004). A comprehensive account of Cook's time in the South Pacific, focusing on a tragic episode in Queen Charlotte Sound in 1777, then widening to encompass many aspects of Cook's voyages.

The Penguin History of New Zealand by Michael King (Penguin Books, 2003). The entire history of New Zealand, from first Polynesian settlement through to the end of the twentieth century, An authoritative and immensely readable account.

Two Worlds: First meetings between Maori and Europeans 1642–1772 by Anne Salmond (Viking, 1991). A ground-breaking work hailed as the first to convey the contacts between European and Maori from a bi-cultural standpoint.

The Captain Cook Encyclopaedia written and edited by John Robson (Random House, 2004). An indispensable reference for anyone interested in Cook's life and voyages. Contains everything from the names of all his crews to a full James Cook bibliography.

The Vaka Moana, Voyagers of the Ancestors: Discovery and settlement of the Pacific edited by Kerry Howe (David Bateman, 2006). Hundreds of years before Cook, Polynesians were carrying out their own exploration of the Pacific Ocean. This is a scholarly account of their remarkable voyages and the navigational techniques they used.

To the Islands: Exploring, remembering, imagining the Hauraki Gulf by Kerry Howe (Mokohinau Islands Press, 2016). Retired academic historian Howe does his own exploration by sea kayak and yacht, of the gulf that Cook passed through in November 1769.

Tupaia: The remarkable story of Captain Cook's Polynesian navigator by Joan Druett (Random House, 2011). Tupaia the priest-navigator from Raiatea in the Leeward Islands, sailed with *Endeavour* to New Zealand and Australia. He proved to be very useful as an emissary between Cook and the Maori.

Hell-Hole of the Pacific by Richard Wolfe (Penguin Books NZ, 2005). A lively account of the Bay of Islands town of Kororareka in the 1830s. Kororareka—today the peaceful town of Russell—was reputed to harbour, 'a greater number of rogues than any other spot of equal size in the universe.'

COMMEMORATING JAMES COOK
IN NEW ZEALAND

The visits of Captain James Cook RN to places throughout New Zealand are commemorated in various ways: by statuary, monuments, cairns and plaques. Some of these are in out-of-the-way places that can be visited only by sea, others have been placed in prominent public spaces.

The first memorial to Cook was erected in 1906, at his initial New Zealand landing place, on the banks of the Turanganui River in Gisborne. There were three other memorials erected before World War II: at Ship Cove and Motuara Island in Queen Charlotte Sound, and in central Christchurch.

The establishment of the New Zealand Historic Places Trust in 1954—renamed Heritage New Zealand Pouhere Taonga in 2014—and the bicentennial of Cook's first visit to New Zealand in 1969, led to a number of other memorials being placed near Cook's landing sites during the second half of the twentieth century. For example, the memorial gates erected at the entrance to Shakespeare Cliff, at Mercury Bay in the Coromandel, commemorate the 1969 Cook bicentenary.

Cook memorials can be seen in the following places throughout New Zealand, from north to south: Motuarohia-Roberton Island (Bay of Islands); Mercury Bay, Kopu and Netherton (Coromandel); Tolaga Bay and Anaura Bay (Tairawhiti); Gisborne city and Wellington city; D'Urville Island, Motuara Island and Ship Cove (in

Queen Charlotte Sound); Christchurch city; and Pickersgill Harbour, in Dusky Sound, Fiordland.

The chapter on Poverty Bay include details of the numerous Cook memorials which can be seen in Gisborne city.

The wording on the commemorative plaques summarise the significance of particular events that occurred there. For example the one at Kopu, in the Coromandel, states, 'Near this spot James Cook with the naturalists Joseph Banks and Daniel Solander landed while exploring the River Thames [now Waihou] in the ship's boats of H.M.S. *Endeavour* 21 November 1769.'

A memorial to this exploratory venture can also be seen at Netherton, on SH 2 inland from Kopu on the Hauraki Plains, near a bend of the Waihou River.

A circular plaque on the walls of Parliament Buildings in New Zealand's capital, Wellington, commemorates the 1769–1969 Cook bicentennial.

A cairn on Motuara Island commemorates the role the island played during Cook's visits to Queen Charlotte Sound, as does the imposing Cook Memorial on the foreshore of Ship Cove. Cook visited the cove on five occasions, as it was his favourite New Zealand anchorage.

A less accessible memorial is a plaque set into the rocky shoreline at Whareatea Bay, on the east coast of D'Urville Island, in Queen Charlotte Sound. The wording on this plaque reads: 'James Cook sailed the *Endeavour* from this bay on 31 March 1770 leaving New Zealand and steering west on his long homeward voyage.' Cook's visit to what was later named D'Urville Island came at the end of his first visit to New Zealand and before his voyage across the Tasman Sea to the east coast of Australia, then known as 'New Holland'.

In Christchurch a marble statue of Cook standing on a granite base, by sculptor William Trethewey, was unveiled in 1932 in Victoria Square in the central city. Thankfully the statue was not damaged by the severe earthquakes that struck Christchurch in 2010 and 2011.

Remote Dusky Sound, in the extreme south-west of the South Island, provided a haven for Cook and the crew of HMS *Resolution* in 1773, during Cook's second world voyage. A plaque is set into the rock at Astronomer's Point, in Pickersgill Harbour, where *Resolution* was moored. There are also information boards nearby stating the historic significance of this site.

Cook placenames abound in New Zealand. The body of water that separates the North Island from the South Island is called Cook Strait and New Zealand's highest mountain, in the heart of the Southern Alps, is binomial Aoraki-Mt Cook (3724 metres). There are streets named after Cook in sixteen towns throughout New Zealand, from Okaihau in Northland to Timpanys in Southland.

Website: www.teara.govt.nz/en/interactive/32558/memorials-to-captain-cook.

Map of Cook memorials in New Zealand

SESTERCENTENNIAL 2019

Sestercentennial: an adjective, pertaining to, or marking the completion of, a period of 250 years.

October 2019 will mark the sestercentennial of James Cook's first arrival in New Zealand and his meetings with Maori in the place they knew as Turanganui and which Cook called Poverty Bay. Today the region is called Tairawhiti-Eastland and its main centre is the city of Gisborne.

In 2014 a trust was launched by the-then Governor General Sir Jerry Mateparae, who stated at the time:

All New Zealanders have a stake in this exciting and meaningful commemoration. It will give us a moment to pause and consider where we come from, the voyaging feats of all our ancestors that ultimately led to our nation's existence, the scientific legacies of our forebears and our understanding of what it means to be a New Zealander.

The Te Ha 1769 Sestercentennial Trust was subsequently formed, for helping plan the 2019 commemorations. Its aims were aspirational. They were for: 'Developing and promoting initiatives enhancing the Eastland region's cultural, social, ecological and economic aspects, and helping create legacies that engender a renewed pride and sense of identity'.

'Te Ha' means 'a sharing of breath'. It derives from the Maori custom, hongi, whereby two people's noses are brought into contact in a gesture of friendship. The Tairawhiti-Eastland region will be the focus of the 2019 commemorations, which should attract a national and international audience.

Three other New Zealand regions were closely associated with James Cook's visits and interactions with local Maori: the Coromandel, the Marlborough Sounds and the Bay of Islands. These areas too have formed trusts on the Te Ha basis and the four are working in unison to commemorate the visit of Cook and *Endeavour* in 1769–70.

The Te Ha trust aims to achieve much more than just a commemoration, however. While the events of 1769–70 are the focus, the sestercentennial should also provide an opportunity to inform and inspire today's youth. It will exemplify the concept of 'Dual Heritage—Shared Future'.

Richard Brooking, chairman of the Te Ha 1769 Sestercentennial Trust says: 'The events are a chance to acknowledge the arrival of all people in Aotearoa-New Zealand and our navigational traditions.'

Another Te Ha trustee, Dame Anne Salmond, Distinguished Professor of Maori Studies and Anthropology at the University of Auckland, summarises the importance of Cook's first meeting with Maori in these words:

The foreshore of the Turanganui River is one of the world's great voyaging sites. It is the landing place of the Horouta canoe, celebrating the achievements of the Polynesian star navigators. It is the place where Captain James Cook and his companions first came ashore in New Zealand, heralding the traditions of European exploration and discovery. It is the site where Tupaia, the Raiatean high priest navigator who sailed with Cook, first met Maori, marking the links between local people and their ancestral homelands. It is a meeting place of cultures, of challenges and shootings, as well as friendly exchanges. Here, Captain Cook and a local man saluted each other with a hongi on Te Toka a Taiau—the first greeting between a Maori and a European. It is a sacred site for all New Zealanders, to be celebrated with pride and treated with dignity. ('Te Ha 1769-2019', *The Gisborne Herald,* 7 October 2015, page 3)

Website: https://gg.govt.nz/content/te-ha-1769-sestercentennial-trust.

THE CAPTAIN COOK SOCIETY

The Society was formed in 1975 as the Captain Cook Study Unit, and changed its name to the current one in 2001. The Captain Cook Society is international, with membership open to anyone with an interest in the life and career of James Cook. Membership numbers have increased steadily over the last few years.

In 2017 the Society's total membership was 553. Of the twenty countries to whom the members belong, the main ones are: the United Kingdom 173, the United States of America 106, Australia 93, New Zealand 72, Canada 52 and Germany 27.

The Society publishes a quarterly, *Cook's Log*, on-line and in hard copy, which is free to all members. This publication contains interesting articles on various aspects of James Cook's life, and the lives of those associated with him. *Cook's Log* publishes features on such subjects as astronomy, Cook books, nautical matters, Cook voyage commemorations, maps, stamps and zoology. The Society's annual subscription rates are £14UK, £28NZ.

The current President of the Captain Cook Society is John Robson, who lives in Hamilton, New Zealand (President@ CaptainCookSociety.com). The Secretary is Alwyn Peel, who lives in Dewsbury, West Yorkshire (Secretary@CaptainCookSociety.com); the Treasurer is Mike Reed of Shefford, Bedfordshire, and the Editor of *Cook's Log* is Ian Boreham of Ipswich, Suffolk (Editor@ CaptainCookSociety.com).

The Cook Society's website is: www.captaincooksociety.com.

ACKNOWLEDGEMENTS

Several people provided me with specialist guidance for this book. I'm grateful for the practical advice of: Captain Cook Society member, John Steele of Whitianga, Paul Carrad , skipper of MV *Pembroke* in Dusky Sound, Anne, Michael and Jeremy Muir of Gisborne, Alicia Caldwell of the Gisborne District Council and Richard Brooking and Te Aturangi Nepia-Clamp of the Te Ha Trust. The staff at the Picton i-SITE Visitors' Centre were also most helpful.

INDEX

S

T

First published in 2017 by New Holland Publishers
London • Sydney • Auckland

newhollandpublishers.com

The Chandlery, 50 Westminster Bridge Road, London SE1 7QY, United Kingdom
1/66 Gibbes Street, Chatswood, NSW 2067, Australia
5/39 Woodside Ave, Northcote, Auckland 0627, New Zealand

Managing Director: David Cowie
Publisher: Christine Thomson
Editor: Liz Hardy
Designer: Catherine Meachen
Production Director: James Mills-Hicks
Printer: Times Printing Malaysia

10 9 8 7 6 5 4 3 2 1

Keep up with New Holland Publishers on Facebook

www.facebook.com/NewHollandPublishers